This book is dedicated to the many outstanding teachers
I've had the pleasure to work with throughout
my career. You've inspired me to be a better teacher,
and I hope this book inspires some great learning
and physical activity in your gym.

Physical Literacy on the Move

Games for Developing Confidence and Competence in Physical Activity

Heather Gardner, MEd

HUMAN KINETICS

Library of Congress Cataloging-in-Publication Data

Names: Gardner, Heather, author.
Title: Physical literacy on the move : games for developing confidence and
    competence in physical activity / Heather Gardner.
Description: Champaign, IL : Human Kinetics, [2017]
Identifiers: LCCN 2016035889| ISBN 9781492535904 (print) | ISBN 9781492547891
    (e-book)
Subjects: LCSH: Physical education and training--Study and teaching. |
    Movement education--Study and teaching. | Individualized instruction.
Classification: LCC GV443 .G36 2017 | DDC 372.86--dc23 LC record available at https://lccn.loc
    .gov/2016035889

ISBN: 978-1-4925-3590-4 (print)

The web addresses cited in this text were current as of December 2016, unless otherwise noted.

Acquisitions Editor: Diana Vincer; **Senior Developmental Editor:** Melissa Feld; **Managing Editor:** Anne E. Mrozek; **Copyeditor:** Patsy Fortney; **Graphic Designer:** Julie L. Denzer; **Cover Designer:** Keith Blomberg; **Photographs (cover):** © Human Kinetics; **Photographs (interior):** © Human Kinetics; **Photo Asset Manager:** Laura Fitch; **Photo Production Manager:** Jason Allen; **Senior Art Manager:** Kelly Hendren; **Illustrations:** © Human Kinetics; **Printer:** Versa Press

Printed in the United States of America   10 9 8 7 6 5 4 3 2 1

The paper in this book is certified under a sustainable forestry program.

Human Kinetics
Website: www.HumanKinetics.com

United States: Human Kinetics
P.O. Box 5076
Champaign, IL 61825-5076
800-747-4457
e-mail: info@hkusa.com

Canada: Human Kinetics
475 Devonshire Road Unit 100
Windsor, ON N8Y 2L5
800-465-7301 (in Canada only)
e-mail: info@hkcanada.com

Europe: Human Kinetics
107 Bradford Road
Stanningley
Leeds LS28 6AT, United Kingdom
+44 (0) 113 255 5665
e-mail: hk@hkeurope.com

E6876

Contents

Game Finder

Game	Page	Level	Fundamental movement skill	Game category
Chapter 1 Low-Organization Games				
Catch It	16	Competent	Throwing underhand, catching	Net/wall
Compliment tag	4	Beginning	Running, dodging	Individual pursuits
Crawling caterpillar	3	Beginning	Balance, coordination	Cooperative games
Don't look	23	Proficient	Coordination	Individual pursuits
Group juggle	26	Proficient	Overhead volley, throwing underhand, catching	Cooperative games
Hive	9	Exploring	Skipping, hopping, running, balance	Cooperative games
Hoop swap	17	Competent	Balance, coordination	Cooperative games
Keep it together	11	Exploring	Running, coordination	Cooperative games
Number slider	24	Proficient	Running	Cooperative games
Stretching shapes	8	Beginning	Balance, coordination	Individual pursuits
Support signals	19	Competent	Running, skipping, hopping	Cooperative games
Toss up	12	Exploring	Throwing underhand, catching	Striking/fielding
Under-the-sea adventure	6	Beginning	Running	Cooperative games
What's the wifi password?	21	Competent	Running	Cooperative games
Zoo sounds	14	Exploring	Running, skipping, hopping	Cooperative games
Chapter 2 Personal Fitness				
ABC fitness	33	Beginning	Running, jumping, skipping	Individual pursuits
Card deck shuffle	31	Beginning	Running	Individual pursuits
Cardio up challenge	47	Competent	Running, jumping, skipping	Individual pursuits
Crazy card relay	51	Competent	Running	Individual pursuits
Dice relay	58	Proficient	Running	Individual pursuits
Double dice fitness stations	45	Competent	Running	Individual pursuits
Fit puzzle relay	36	Beginning	Running	Individual pursuits
Four-corner components of fitness	55	Proficient	Running, jumping, skipping, coordination	Individual pursuits
Laps	43	Exploring	Running, jumping, skipping	Individual pursuits
Line race	53	Proficient	Coordination	Individual pursuits
Rock-paper-scissors baseball	56	Proficient	Running, skipping, coordination	Individual pursuits

(continued ►►)

Game	Page	Level	Fundamental movement skill	Game category
Chapter 2 Personal Fitness ►►				
Rock-paper-scissors rotation	49	Competent	Coordination	Individual pursuits
Run and roll	41	Exploring	Running	Individual pursuits
Suits	38	Exploring	Running, jumping, skipping	Individual pursuits
Yoga zoo	40	Exploring	Balance	Individual pursuits
Chapter 3 Gymnastics				
Balance shapes	79	Exploring	Balance	Individual pursuits
Balance slow-down cool-down	87	Competent	Balance	Individual pursuits
Balance tag	69	Beginning	Agility, balance, running	Individual pursuits
Bench balance stations	73	Exploring	Balance	Individual pursuits
Dice roll balance	67	Beginning	Balance	Individual pursuits
Flash card balance	65	Beginning	Balance	Individual pursuits
Four-corner partner balance	75	Exploring	Balance	Individual pursuits
Lean on me	88	Proficient	Balance, running, skipping, jumping	Individual pursuits
Line jump	77	Exploring	Jumping, running, skipping	Individual pursuits
Locomotor hoopla	83	Competent	Running, jumping, skipping	Individual pursuits
Mirroring movements	81	Competent	Running, skipping, jumping, balance	Individual pursuits
Movement stations on and off equipment	85	Competent	Balance, coordination	Individual pursuits
Rock and roll	71	Beginning	Coordination	Individual pursuits
Rotation stations	92	Proficient	Coordination	Individual pursuits
You or me	90	Proficient	Balance	Individual pursuits
Chapter 4 Creative Movement				
Add up moves	107	Beginning	Agility, balance, coordination, running, jumping	Individual pursuits
Bend, stretch, twist, turn, meet, part	125	Proficient	Agility, balance, coordination	Individual pursuits
Can you . . .	103	Beginning	Agility, coordination	Individual pursuits
Comic book moves	121	Competent	Agility, balance, coordination, running, jumping	Individual pursuits

Game	Page	Level	Fundamental movement skill	Game category
Chapter 4 Creative Movement ▸▸				
Dance add-on	130	Proficient	Agility, balance, coordination, running, jumping	Individual pursuits
Dance replacement	126	Proficient	Agility, balance, coordination, running, jumping	Individual pursuits
Exploring direction dance stations	113	Exploring	Agility, balance, coordination	Individual pursuits
Four-way dance-off	111	Exploring	Agility, balance, coordination	Individual pursuits
In pursuit	128	Proficient	Agility, balance, coordination, running, jumping	Individual pursuits
Moving a round	115	Exploring	Agility, coordination, jumping	Individual pursuits
Moving triangle	119	Competent	Agility, balance, coordination, running, jumping	Individual pursuits
Partner moves	117	Competent	Agility, coordination	Individual pursuits
Statues	123	Competent	Agility, balance, coordination	Individual pursuits
Storybook movements	109	Exploring	Agility, balance, coordination, running, jumping	Individual pursuits
Which part leads?	105	Beginning	Agility, coordination, running, jumping	Individual pursuits
Chapter 5 Running and Skipping				
10-meter dash	144	Exploring	Running	Individual pursuits
Aliens and astronauts	143	Exploring	Running	Individual pursuits
At the race track	140	Beginning	Running	Individual pursuits
Cat in a tree	138	Beginning	Skipping, balance	Individual pursuits
Couch potato tag	148	Exploring	Running	Individual pursuits
Even steven	157	Proficient	Running	Individual pursuits
If, you run	146	Exploring	Running	Individual pursuits
Rabbit run	161	Proficient	Running	Individual pursuits
Relay run	149	Exploring	Running	Individual pursuits
Run across the world	156	Competent	Running	Individual pursuits
Shadow tag	141	Beginning	Skipping	Individual pursuits
Smoothie tag	154	Competent	Skipping	Individual pursuits
Snail and deer tag	153	Competent	Skipping	Individual pursuits
Speedy leader	151	Competent	Running	Individual pursuits
Tag team	159	Proficient	Skipping	Individual pursuits

(continued ▸▸)

Game	Page	Level	Fundamental movement skill	Game category
Chapter 6 Throwing and Catching				
Around the bases	191	Proficient	Throwing underhand and overhand, catching	Striking/fielding
Basketball golf	181	Competent	Throwing underhand and overhand	Target
Beanbag curling	189	Proficient	Throwing underhand	Target
Catch and run	173	Beginning	Throwing underhand, catching	Striking/fielding
Catch around	176	Exploring	Throwing underhand and overhand, catching	Territory
Disc landing	174	Exploring	Throwing backhand	Target
End ball	188	Proficient	Throwing underhand and overhand, catching	Territory
Knock out	193	Proficient	Throwing underhand and overhand, catching	Territory
Noodle archery	179	Exploring	Throwing overhand	Target
On the run	171	Beginning	Throwing underhand, catching, running	Striking/fielding
Rolled over	168	Beginning	Throwing underhand	Target
Spell it	177	Exploring	Throwing underhand and overhand, catching	Territory
Star toss	183	Proficient	Throwing underhand and overhand, catching	Striking/fielding
Target tip-over	169	Beginning	Throwing underhand	Target
Throw volleyball	184	Competent	Throwing underhand and overhand, catching	Net/wall
Ultimate football	186	Competent	Kicking, throwing, catching	Territory
Chapter 7 Striking With Hands				
Blocker	220	Proficient	Overhead volleying	Net/wall
Crazy eights	215	Competent	Overhead volleying	Net/wall
Dice roll keep-away	209	Competent	Dribbling	Territory
Dribble tag	200	Beginning	Dribbling	Territory
Four-pass basketball	222	Proficient	Dribbling	Territory
Freeze count	202	Beginning	Dribbling	Territory
Keep it up	214	Competent	Overhead volleying	Net/wall
Multiball beach ball volleyball	205	Exploring	Overhead volleying	Territory
Pass through	203	Exploring	Dribbling	Territory
Sideline basketball	219	Proficient	Dribbling	Territory

Game	Page	Level	Fundamental movement skill	Game category
Chapter 7 Striking With Hands ▸▸				
Sitting volleyball	217	Proficient	Overhead volleying	Net/wall
Triangles	210	Competent	Overhead volleying	Net/wall
Umbrella drill	212	Competent	Overhead volleying	Net/wall
Volley up and run	207	Exploring	Overhead volleying	Territory
Volley with love	199	Beginning	Overhead volleying	Net/wall
Chapter 8 Striking With an Implement or Feet				
Blade targets	234	Beginning	Striking with an implement	Territory
Captive hockey	253	Proficient	Striking, dribbling, trapping	Territory
Five-minute mini-game	246	Competent	Kicking, dribbling, trapping	Territory
Give-and-go	242	Exploring	Kicking, dribbling, trapping	Territory
Hockey circle relay	232	Beginning	Striking with an implement, running	Territory
Hold fast	248	Competent	Striking with an implement, trapping	Territory
Kicking star	237	Exploring	Kicking	Territory
One-end soccer	240	Exploring	Kicking, dribbling, trapping	Territory
Short- and long-base kick baseball	245	Competent	Kicking	Striking/fielding
Squared out	235	Beginning	Dribbling	Territory
Team croquet	238	Exploring	Striking with an implement	Target
Uneven keep-away	243	Competent	Kicking, dribbling, trapping	Territory
Wall ball soccer	250	Proficient	Kicking, dribbling, trapping	Territory
Zone ringette	251	Proficient	Striking, dribbling, trapping	Territory

Acknowledgments

Active kids become active adults. Thank you to my parents, Jill and Peter Rumble, for instilling in me a love of physical activity and movement; for teaching me that physical activity is fun; and for lighting my passion to inspire movement and healthy living in children, youths, and adults.

Thank you to Debbie Sprentz, Myra Stephen, and Brenda Whitteker, three wonderful leaders in education who guided and supported me through various stages of my career. You have provided me with opportunities to find my voice outside the classroom—throughout the Hamilton-Wentworth District School Board, across Ontario, and across Canada—and have been invaluable role models.

Special thanks to Andrea Haefele and Allison Larouche, wonderful educators whom I've had the pleasure to work with for years and get to know as friends. Thank you for sharing your expert eyes, creative hearts, and professional knowledge, and for guiding me along this writing journey with your questions and feedback.

Thank you to my husband, Mark, for being a great source of support and encouragement throughout this writing process and life. Thank you for your patience so I could make my deadlines, and for keeping the writing process fun by sharing your hilarious activity ideas, including the ones that would never have made the cut. xo

And special thanks to all of you awesome educators who have bought this book and are putting it to use—wearing down the pages, folding the corners, and doing what it takes to promote healthy, active living in the children and youths you work with.

Introduction

Physical Literacy on the Move was written to help educators of children and youths from grades K through 12 teach high-quality and fun games and activities that support the unique needs of their learners as they develop physical literacy. This comprehensive theory-into-practice resource presents 120 ready-to-use games and activities that require minimal equipment and can take place in a variety of settings. They are organized into eight chapters to facilitate quick instructional preparation: Low-Organization Games, Personal Fitness, Gymnastics, Creative Movement, Running and Skipping, Throwing and Catching, Striking With Hands, and Striking With an Implement or Feet. Each activity includes adaptations to either increase or decrease the challenge. Activities conclude with self-check questions related to the movement skills, concepts, and strategies addressed, as well as living skills such as relationship, social, and critical thinking skills.

What Is Physical Literacy?

Physical and Health Education Canada defines physically literate people as those who "move with competence and confidence in a wide variety of physical activities in multiple environments that benefit the healthy development of the whole person" (www.phecanada.ca/programs/physical-literacy). The definition continues as follows:

- Physically literate individuals consistently develop the motivation and ability to understand, communicate, apply, and analyze different forms of movement.

- They are able to demonstrate a variety of movements confidently, competently, creatively, and strategically across a wide range of health-related physical activities.

- These skills enable individuals to make healthy, active choices that are both beneficial to and respectful of their whole self, others, and their environment.

The games and activities in *Physical Literacy on the Move* help participants at various skill levels and from grades K through 12 develop the competence and confidence they need to live healthy, active lives. This book goes beyond instructing sport skills, drills, and fitness training into incorporating a holistic approach to physical literacy instruction. This approach includes learning fundamental movement skills and strategies through games and activities as well as exploring individual pursuits such as creative movement, gymnastics, and low-organization games.

Keeping Learning Fun With Participant Choice

Educators using this book act as facilitators while participants choose their own groups, equipment, game setups, and adaptations to optimize the challenge and maximize the participation and fun. Educator flexibility is key in creating a learning environment where participants may experiment with personal choices in order to work at their optimal level of challenge. Allowing participants to select the type, color, or size of equipment; the size of the playing area or net; the distance from the target; or the scoring scheme, gives participants of all skill levels the opportunity to have their personal needs met while learning with others in the same activity space. A variety of adaptations follow each activity to provide opportunities for learners to work within their own levels of physical literacy in a shared learning environment.

Organization

Physical Literacy on the Move is based on a holistic view of physical literacy. Key concepts are presented according to a learner-centered and skill-based progression, acknowledging that quality instruction is connected to learners' needs as well as their stages of physical and emotional development. Fundamental movement skill development is age related but not age dependent, and physical ability depends on factors such as experience, including that with clubs or teams; personal rate of development; and interests. The games and activities in this book are grouped into four progressive levels of learning: beginning, exploring, competent, and proficient. This permits educators to support learners' individual needs so they can work within their unique levels of optimal challenge.

Beginning (Ages 4–8, Grades K–3)

The beginning category presents developmentally appropriate fundamental movement skills and simple strategies through games and activities suitable for children ages 4 through 8 (kindergarten to grade 3), or for children or youths at lower developmental or experiential levels (see table I.1).

Table I.1 Beginning Category: Fundamental Movement Skills and Strategies

Fundamental movement skills	Strategies explored in the beginning category
Agility Balance Coordination Dodging Running Jumping Skipping Throwing underhand Catching Striking with hands Striking with an implement Kicking Trapping	• Close proximity to target (target) • Consistency—offensive (net/wall) • Defending space—defensive (net/wall) • Moving quickly to score runs—offensive (striking/fielding) • Stopping runs from scoring—defensive (striking/fielding) • Maintaining possession—offensive (territory) • Defending space—defensive (territory) • Traveling through space demonstrating appropriate movement concepts (individual pursuits) • Understanding personal areas of strength and need for improvement (individual pursuits) • Applying appropriate movement skills (individual pursuits) • Developing and applying appropriate movement strategies (individual pursuits) • Using appropriate body parts (individual pursuits) • Demonstrating controlled movements (individual pursuits) • Working collaboratively with teammates (individual pursuits) • Moving safely throughout the activity space (individual pursuits) • Demonstrating fair play (individual pursuits) • Applying strategies to avoid being tagged (individual pursuits) • Applying problem-solving skills (individual pursuits) • Working at an optimal challenge level by using personal tactics (individual pursuits)

Exploring (Ages 9–11, Grades 4–6)

The exploring category highlights developmentally appropriate movement skills and novice strategies through games and activities suitable for children ages 9 through 11 (grades 4 through 6), for older children who require leveled-down skills and activities, or for younger children who require more challenging activities and games (see table I.2).

Table I.2 Exploring Category: Fundamental Movement Skills and Strategies

Fundamental movement skills	Strategies explored in the exploring category
Running Hopping Jumping Skipping Throwing underhand Throwing overhand Throwing backhand Kicking Striking with hands Striking with an implement Catching Trapping	• Close proximity to target—offensive (target) • Avoiding obstacles—offensive (target) • Setting up for an attack—offensive (net/wall) • Defend space—defensive (net/wall) • Defending against an attack—defensive (net/wall) • Consistency—offensive (net/wall) • Stopping runs from scoring—defensive (striking/fielding) • Moving quickly to score runs—offensive (striking/fielding) • Maintaining possession—offensive (territory) • Regaining possession—defensive (territory) • Creating space—offensive (territory) • Attacking the goal—offensive (territory) • Defending the goal—defensive (territory) • Applying appropriate movement skills (individual pursuits) • Using appropriate body parts (individual pursuits) • Working collaboratively with teammates (individual pursuits) • Moving safely throughout the activity space (individual pursuits) • Applying strategies to avoid being tagged (individual pursuits) • Applying problem-solving skills (individual pursuits) • Working at an optimal challenge level by using personal tactics (individual pursuits)

Competent (Ages 12–15, Grades 7–10)

The competent category highlights developmentally appropriate movement skills and intermediate strategies through games and activities suitable for learners ages 12 through 15 (grades 7 through 10), for those who require leveled-down skills and activities, or for younger children who require more challenging activities and games (see table I.3).

Table I.3 Competent Category: Fundamental Movement Skills and Strategies

Fundamental movement skills	Strategies explored in the competent category
Agility Balance Coordination Running Jumping Skipping Throwing underhand Throwing overhand Kicking Striking with hands Striking with an implement Catching Trapping	• Avoiding obstacles—offensive (target) • Creating a dynamic reaction—offensive (target) • Consistency—offensive (net/wall) • Setting up for an attack—offensive (net/wall) • Defending against an attack—defensive (net/wall) • Avoiding getting out—offensive (striking/fielding) • Making hitting the ball difficult—defensive (striking/fielding) • Stopping runs from scoring runs—defensive (striking/fielding) • Moving quickly to score runs—offensive (striking/fielding) • Maintaining possession—offensive (territory) • Regaining possession—defensive (territory) • Creating space—offensive (territory) • Attacking the goal—offensive (territory) • Defending the goal—defensive (territory) • Setting plays—defensive (territory) • Understanding personal areas of strength and need for improvement (individual pursuits) • Applying appropriate movement skills (individual pursuits) • Developing and applying appropriate strategies (individual pursuits) • Communicating effectively and working collaboratively with teammates (individual pursuits) • Moving safely throughout the activity space (individual pursuits) • Applying strategies to avoid being tagged (individual pursuits) • Applying problem-solving skills (individual pursuits)

Proficient (Ages 16 and 17, Grades 11 and 12)

The proficient category highlights developmentally appropriate movement skills and complex strategies through games and activities suitable for youths ages 16 and 17 (grades 11 and 12) or for those in the exploring ages who may require more challenging skills and activities (see table I.4).

In learner-centered games and activities that focus on individual needs related to movement skills, movement concepts, and movement strategies, participants make choices that empower them to explore and develop physical literacy while enjoying being physically active now and throughout their lives.

Table I.4 Proficient Category: Fundamental Movement Skills and Strategies

Fundamental movement skills	Strategies explored in the proficient category
Agility Balance Coordination Running Jumping Skipping Throwing underhand Throwing overhand Striking with hands Kicking Striking with an implement Catching Trapping	• Creating a dynamic reaction—offensive (target) • Avoiding obstacles—offensive (target) • Getting the last shot—offensive (target) • Winning the point—offensive (net/wall) • Defending against an attack—defensive (net/wall) • Setting up an attack—offensive (net/wall) • Regaining possession—defensive (net/wall) • Maintaining possession—offensive (net/wall) • Stopping runs from scoring—defensive (striking/fielding) • Avoiding getting out—offensive (striking/fielding) • Moving quickly to score runs—offensive (striking/fielding) • Creating space—offensive (territory) • Attacking the goal—offensive (territory) • Setting plays—defensive (territory) • Defending the goal—defensive (territory) • Regaining possession—defensive (territory) • Maintaining possession—offensive (territory) • Understanding personal areas of strength and need for improvement (individual pursuits) • Applying appropriate movement skills (individual pursuits) • Developing and applying appropriate strategies (individual pursuits) • Coordinating appropriate body parts during movement (individual pursuits) • Working collaboratively with teammates (individual pursuits) • Moving safely throughout the activity space (individual pursuits) • Applying strategies to avoid being tagged (individual pursuits) • Applying problem-solving skills (individual pursuits)

Navigating the Chapter Overview

Each chapter begins with the following sections:

- **Words to Know.** A glossary of terms as well as illustrations important to physical literacy instruction focused on the fundamental movement skills addressed.

- **Where's the Physical Literacy?** Background information and other key learning connected to fundamental movement skills, movement concepts, and movement strategies.

- **Educator Check and Reflect.** Teaching and safety tips, strategies for creating an inclusive learning environment, and reminders for educators.

Navigating the Activities and Games

All of the games and activities in this book are presented using the following template:

- **Activity Goal.** Objectives and goals presented using participant-friendly language.

- **Fundamental Movement Skill(s).** The fundamental movement skill(s) explored in the game or activity.

- **Tactical Focus.** Strategies participants might use to succeed in the activity or game.

- **Level.** One of the four suggested developmental levels.

- **Facility.** Possible location for the instruction.

- **Equipment.** Required materials and equipment for the activity or game.

- **Time.** A suggested range of time for the activity, not including setup.

- **Activity Category.** Teaching Games for Understanding (TGfU) game category with the addition of individual pursuits to group games with common features (e.g., rules, skills, and strategies).

- **Safety.** General safety considerations (refer to your facility or organization's safety requirements for all activities).

- **Activity Instructions.** Instructions for teaching and setting up the game or activity. Small groups are suggested to maximize participation. Learner choice is encouraged to promote fun and engagement.

- **Adaptations.** Adaptations to create an optimal challenge, including suggestions for both decreasing and increasing the challenge of the game or activity. Use your professional judgement and knowledge of your participants to create an optimal learning environment.

- **Self-Check Questions.** Personal reflection questions that participants can complete during or following the activity. Participants analyze their knowledge or application of the skill or strategy used throughout the game or activity. Questions are developmentally appropriate based on the skills and strategies explored. The questions can act as a self- or peer assessment tool, or simply as a pause in which participants can reflect on new skills and strategies to try.

Using the Game Finder

The game finder at the beginning of the book can be used to locate activities and games quickly and easily. The games and activities in each chapter are listed alphabetically along with their developmental levels, fundamental movement skills, and categories.

Now, let's move!

Low-Organization Games

This chapter addresses cooperation, inclusion, and fun while promoting team success through the application of interpersonal skills as well as critical and creative thinking skills. Participants demonstrate a variety of fundamental movement skills in partner and small-group challenges, relays, parachute activities, and tag games that emphasize participation, challenge, and fun rather than competition.

Words to Know

- **Communication skills.** Skills that result in the transfer of information from one person to another; they include both verbal and nonverbal skills such as body language.
- **Critical and creative thinking skills.** The ability to think clearly about how to respond in a given situation; these skills include observation, analysis, inference, evaluation, and explanation.
- **Relationship and social skills.** Skills that facilitate interactions with others, including working collaboratively, playing fairly, and respecting differences.

Where's the Physical Literacy?

Low-organization games provide the opportunity to interact with others in unique ways while developing interpersonal skills including verbal and nonverbal communication skills (e.g., receiving, interpreting, sending information), relationship and social skills (e.g., demonstrating fair play and teamwork, showing respect for others, appreciating others' differences), and critical and creative thinking skills (e.g., organizing information, analyzing, evaluating, and deciding). While exploring a variety of fundamental movement skills (e.g., running, skipping, hopping, throwing, catching, striking with hands, balancing, and exhibiting coordination), participants interact and collaborate with each other while building community and developing healthy relationships. Through cooperative games, participants explore movement skills in an inclusive and supportive environment in which they develop a sense of belonging and demonstrate respect for their own abilities and those of others.

Educator Check and Reflect

- Consider using these low-organization games at the start of a new term or year to develop an inclusive and welcoming learning environment.
- Establish an emotionally safe learning environment.
- Stop and switch teams if one team is dominating the activity.
- Maximize participation by using smaller teams.
- Highlight and praise moments in which participants demonstrate cooperation and fair play.

Activity Goal

To work cooperatively with teammates to move one's team a certain distance across the activity space.

Fundamental Movement Skills

Balance, coordination

Tactical Focus

- Demonstrate controlled movement skills to safely travel through the activity area.
- Work collaboratively with teammates.

Level

Beginning

Facility

Gymnasium or outdoors

Equipment

None

Time

15 to 20 minutes

Activity Category

Cooperative games

Safety

Ensure that indoor and outdoor activity spaces are a safe distance from walls and free of hazards (e.g., benches, equipment, basketball nets, holes, loose gravel, wet grass); remove or mark any hazards. Provide safe distances between games occurring in the same space. Remind participants to keep their heads up and to be aware of others when moving through the space.

Activity Instructions

Divide participants into groups of five. At one end of the gym, groups lie on the floor in a line with each person's hands touching the feet of the person in front. Groups attempt to move together as one long caterpillar and see how far they can go without coming apart.

Adaptations

To decrease the challenge:

- Reduce the number of people per group.
- Reduce the distance the group must travel.
- Allow groups a number of opportunities to come apart.

To increase the challenge:

- Increase the number of people per group.
- Increase the distance the group needs to travel.
- Do not allow group members to speak.
- Have groups move over and around pieces of equipment (e.g., over a bench, through a hula hoop).

Self-Check Questions

- Am I communicating well with my group?
- Am I showing respect for my group?
- Am I participating safely in my group?

COMPLIMENT TAG

Activity Goal

To attempt to tag as many players as possible or to avoid being tagged.

Fundamental Movement Skills

Running, dodging

Tactical Focus

- Demonstrate locomotor movements safely in the activity area.
- Apply strategies to avoid being tagged, or to tag others.
- Demonstrate fair play by following the rules.

Level
Beginning

Facility
Gymnasium or outdoors

Equipment
None

Time
15 to 20 minutes

Activity Category
Individual pursuits

Safety
Ensure that indoor and outdoor activity spaces are a safe distance from walls and free of hazards (e.g., benches, equipment, basketball nets, holes, loose gravel, wet grass); remove or mark any hazards. Remind participants to keep their heads up and to be aware of others when moving through the space.

Activity Instructions
Three to five participants volunteer to be taggers. Identify taggers with markers (e.g., pinnies, gloves, bandanas, fake flower lei necklaces). Participants move throughout the space trying to tag and to avoid being tagged.

Tagged participants must freeze with one hand held high. To free a tagged player, a free player must high-five the frozen player's hand and offer a compliment. Change taggers often.

Adaptations
To decrease the challenge:
- Increase the size of the playing area.
- Allow taggers to use an implement (e.g., pool noodles) to tag.

To increase the challenge:
- Change the way the participants must travel (e.g., skip, gallop, hop).
- Decrease the size of the playing area.

Self-Check Questions

- Am I moving safely in the activity area?
- Am I applying strategies to avoid being tagged, or to tag others?
- Do I demonstrate fair play by following the rules?

UNDER-THE-SEA ADVENTURE

Activity Goal

To work cooperatively with others while moving with and under a parachute.

Fundamental Movement Skill

Running

Tactical Focus

- Demonstrate locomotor movements safely around and under the parachute.
- Demonstrate fair play by following the rules and working cooperatively with others.

Level

Beginning

Facility

Gymnasium or outdoors

Equipment

Parachute

Time

15 to 20 minutes

Activity Category

Cooperative games

Safety

Ensure that indoor and outdoor activity spaces are a safe distance from walls and free of hazards (e.g., benches, equipment, basketball nets, holes, loose gravel, wet grass); remove or mark any hazards. Remind participants to keep their heads up and to be aware of others when moving through the space.

Activity Instructions

Participants sit evenly spaced around a parachute. As directed, participants make small, medium, or large movements to create ocean waves.

Divide participants into four groups and give each an aquatic-themed name (e.g., starfish, whales, jellyfish, seahorses). Have group members spread out around the parachute and make small, medium, or large waves. As each group name is called, group members swim under the ocean (parachute) to empty spaces on the other side.

Adaptations

To decrease the challenge:

- Have participants travel under the parachute in pairs.
- Have participants wave the parachute using handles.
- Have participants roll a ball to a partner on the other side of the parachute rather than travel underneath it.

To increase the challenge:

- Choose one participant to be a shark and stay under the parachute. When a group is called, the shark tries to take one of the open spaces. The participant without a space becomes the new shark.
- Set a time limit for participants to move under the parachute.
- Have participants wave the parachute with their nondominant hands.

Self-Check Questions

- Am I moving safely around and under the parachute?
- Do I demonstrate fair play by following the rules?

STRETCHING SHAPES

Activity Goal

To work cooperatively with teammates to create shapes.

Fundamental Movement Skills

Balance, coordination

Tactical Focus

Apply problem-solving skills while working collaboratively to create shapes.

Level

Beginning

Facility

Gymnasium or outdoors

Equipment

Shape cards (optional)

Time

15 to 20 minutes

Activity Category

Individual pursuits

Safety

Ensure that indoor and outdoor activity spaces are a safe distance from walls and free of hazards (e.g., benches, equipment, basketball nets, holes, loose gravel, wet grass); remove or mark any hazards. Provide safe distances between activities occurring in the same space. Remind participants to keep their heads up and to be aware of others when moving through the space.

Activity Instructions

Divide participants into groups of five or six. For each group, call out a shape and hold up a card with the shape on it. Group members work together to stretch their bodies into the shape, either lying down or standing up. Consider using shapes participants are familiar with from math instruction.

Adaptations

To decrease the challenge:

- Use simple shapes participants are familiar with.
- Provide each group with a copy of the card that shows the shape.

To increase the challenge:

- Have participants work with their eyes closed.
- Do not allow group members to talk to each other.
- Present intricate shapes that have many angles.

Self-Check Questions

- Am I communicating well with my group mates?
- Am I showing respect for my group mates?
- Do I apply critical thinking skills to solve problems with my group?

HIVE

Activity Goal

To move together as a team and, on a signal, apply critical thinking skills to fit together into a hoop.

Fundamental Movement Skills

Skipping, hopping, running, balance

Tactical Focus

- Work collaboratively with teammates to fit into the hoop.
- Apply problem-solving skills with teammates to fit into the hoop.

Level

Exploring

Facility

Gymnasium or outdoors

Equipment

8 to 10 hula hoops or mats

Time

15 to 20 minutes

Activity Category

Cooperative games

Safety

Ensure that indoor and outdoor activity spaces are a safe distance from walls and free of hazards (e.g., benches, equipment, basketball nets, holes, loose gravel, wet grass); remove or mark any hazards. Provide safe distances between hoops. Remind participants to keep their heads up and to be aware of others when moving through the space.

Activity Instructions

Prior to the activity, scatter 8 to 10 hula hoops or gymnasium mats around the activity space. These are the bee hives.

Divide participants into groups of four or five. Groups travel together around the activity space as directed (e.g., walk, skip, hop, jog). When you call out "Honey time," each group moves to the closest hoop or mat and all participants try to fit into the hoop or onto the mat. Repeat the activity, each time removing one hoop or mat. More than one group can be on each hoop or mat, and groups should work together to include all members.

Adaptations

To decrease the challenge:

- Use larger hoops or mats.
- Create smaller groups.
- Offer no time limit on the activity.

To increase the challenge:

- Use smaller hoops or mats.
- Provide a time limit for fitting into the hoop or onto the mat.

Self-Check Questions

- Am I communicating well with my group mates?
- Am I contributing to the success of my group?
- Do I demonstrate critical thinking skills while solving problems with my group?

Activity Goal

To move the group across the activity area while staying connected.

Fundamental Movement Skills

Running, coordination

Tactical Focus

- Work collaboratively to safely travel through the space together.
- Use appropriate body parts to move in a specific direction and at a certain speed with the group.

Level

Exploring

Facility

Gymnasium with lines (e.g., basketball or badminton court)

Equipment

None

Time

15 to 20 minutes

Activity Category

Cooperative games

Safety

Ensure that indoor and outdoor activity spaces are a safe distance from walls and free of hazards (e.g., benches, equipment, basketball nets, holes, loose gravel, wet grass); remove or mark any hazards. Remind participants to keep their heads up and to be aware of others when moving through the space.

Activity Instructions

Divide participants into groups of five or six and have them stand side by side with shoulders touching. All groups begin at one end of the activity space and travel along the floor lines to the opposite end of the activity area. Groups that break contact must start again. Next, participants move while making contact with other parts of the body (e.g., elbows, backs of hands, fingertips, outside edges of feet).

Adaptations

To decrease the challenge:

- Have groups move in their own spaces (not using gym lines) to get to the other end of the activity area.
- Decrease the number of participants per group.

To increase the challenge:

- Set a time frame in which participants must complete the task.
- Have participants travel through an obstacle course (e.g., over a bench, through a hoop).
- Increase the number of participants per group.

Self-Check Questions

- Am I communicating well with my group mates?
- Am I showing respect for my group mates?
- Am I applying critical thinking skills to help my group solve problems?

TOSS UP

Activity Goal

To work as a team to catch and throw an object.

Fundamental Movement Skills

Throwing underhand, catching

Tactical Focus

- Offense: Score points; apply appropriate movement skills to throw the object.
- Defense: Stop opponents from scoring points; work collaboratively on a team to catch an object; apply appropriate movement skills to catch the object.

Level

Exploring

Facility

Gymnasium or outdoors

Equipment

5 or 6 plush objects (per group)

Time

15 to 20 minutes

Activity Category

Striking/fielding

Safety

Ensure that indoor and outdoor activity spaces are a safe distance from walls and free of hazards (e.g., benches, equipment, basketball nets, holes, loose gravel, wet grass); remove or mark any hazards. Provide safe distances between games occurring in the same space. Remind participants to keep their heads up and to be aware of others when moving through the space.

Activity Instructions

Divide participants into teams of six to eight, which then pair up to compete. Each team pair begins with one plush object. When you call out "Toss up," a participant on one team throws the object straight up (8 to 10 ft, or 2.5 to 3 m) and that team performs a task (e.g., jumping jack, squat, calf raise), counting the repetitions out loud until the object is caught or retrieved by someone on the other team, who then shouts "Stop."

The throwing group receives points for the number of times the members performed the task (e.g., 10 jumping jacks = 10 points). A second object is added if the object was caught before hitting the floor. The activity is repeated, this time with the other team throwing the second object simultaneously with the first. Both objects need to be retrieved by the other team to stop the group from collecting points. If the objects are caught before hitting the ground, another object is added and the game continues.

Adaptations

To decrease the challenge:

- Reduce the required height of the throw.
- Allow groups to choose which members will catch and which will perform the physical task.

- Use objects that are easier to catch (e.g., larger, brighter, with handles to grab).

To increase the challenge:

- Increase the required height of the throw.
- Decrease the size of the object.
- Use objects that are more difficult to catch (e.g., rubber chickens, objects with uneven weighting).

Self-Check Questions

- Am I communicating well and showing respect for my teammates?
- Do I demonstrate fair play by following the rules?
- Can I apply appropriate movement skills when throwing and catching an object?

ZOO SOUNDS

Activity Goal

To demonstrate a variety of locomotor movements while imitating the sounds of zoo animals to create a group.

Fundamental Movement Skills

Running, skipping, hopping

Tactical Focus

- Work collaboratively with group mates.
- Demonstrate a variety of locomotor movements while traveling safely.

Level

Exploring

Facility

Gymnasium or outdoors

Equipment

None

Time

15 to 20 minutes

Activity Category

Cooperative games

Safety

Ensure that indoor and outdoor activity spaces are a safe distance from walls and free of hazards (e.g., benches, equipment, basketball nets, holes, loose gravel, wet grass); remove or mark any hazards. Remind participants to keep their heads up and to be aware of others when moving through the space.

Activity Instructions

Assign each participant a secret zoo animal that makes a sound (e.g., elephant, lion, snake). On your signal (e.g., whistle, clap, "Go"), participants travel around the activity space making the noise of their assigned animals and searching for others of the same kind. Encourage participants to travel using a variety of locomotor movements (e.g., skip, hop, jump, gallop). Animals of the same type travel together until all participants have found their animal groups. Once formed, groups perform the same task until all participants have found their groups. Change animals and repeat the activity.

Adaptations

To decrease the challenge:

- Display illustrations of animals throughout the activity space for reference.
- Have participants work in pairs.
- Reduce the intensity of the tasks.

To increase the challenge:

- Reduce the number of participants for each type of animal.
- Increase the intensity of the tasks.
- Have participants line up across the activity space from a partner. With closed eyes, participants carefully walk across the space making animal noises to find their partners. Ensure that participants move safely and cautiously.

Self-Check Questions

- Am I communicating well with my partner?
- Am I moving safely throughout the activity space?
- Do I demonstrate fair play by following the rules?

CATCH IT

Activity Goal

To complete consecutive catches after one bounce while working with a partner.

Fundamental Movement Skills

Throwing underhand, catching

Tactical Focus

- Demonstrate movement skills while attempting to catch a bounced ball.
- Work collaboratively with a partner to catch a ball.

Level

Competent

Facility

Gymnasium or outdoors

Equipment

1 bouncy ball per pair

Time

20 to 25 minutes

Activity Category

Net/wall

Safety

Ensure that indoor and outdoor activity spaces are a safe distance from walls and free of hazards (e.g., benches, equipment, basketball nets, holes, loose gravel, wet grass); remove or mark any hazards. Provide safe distances between pairs. Remind participants to keep their heads up and to be aware of other pairs and balls moving around the space.

Activity Instructions

Divide participants into pairs with one partner standing on one side of a line. Participants take turns bouncing the ball on their side of the court, so that partners can catch it in the air on their own sides. Pairs count the number of consecutive passes.

After an appropriate amount of time, consider having pairs take one step away from each other for every pass caught. Participants who miss a catch return to their original spots.

Adaptations

To decrease the challenge:

- Allow more than one bounce.
- Decrease the size of the playing area.
- Have participants work in teams of four.

To increase the challenge:

- Increase the size of the playing area.
- Add a net.
- Have participants play against a wall.
- Change the direction, speed, and height of the ball.

Self-Check Questions

- Am I communicating well with my partner?
- Am I anticipating my partner's moves?
- Am I applying appropriate force considering the position of my partner?

HOOP SWAP

Activity Goal

To solve problems with group mates while changing positions inside a line of hula hoops.

Fundamental Movement Skills

Balance, coordination

Tactical Focus

- Communicate with group mates while working out the positioning within the hula hoops.
- Work collaboratively with group mates to move through the hula hoops

Level

Competent

Facility

Gymnasium or outdoors

Equipment

1 hula hoop for every participant, with 1 extra for each group of 8 to 10

Time

15 to 20 minutes

Activity Category

Cooperative games

Safety

Ensure that indoor and outdoor activity spaces are a safe distance from walls and free of hazards (e.g., benches, equipment, basketball nets, holes, loose gravel, wet grass); remove or mark any hazards. Provide safe distances between activities occurring in the same space. Remind participants to keep their heads up and to be aware of others when moving through the space.

Activity Instructions

Divide participants into groups of 8 to 10, and give each group a hula hoop for each member, plus one extra. Groups place their hula hoops in a straight line with the empty hoop near the middle of the line. Each participant stands in a hoop, and they work together to reverse their order within the line of hoops (participants at the front move to the back, and vice versa). Participants may not step outside of the hoops. Those that do must return to their original positions.

Adaptations

To decrease the challenge:

- Provide additional empty hoops.
- Increase the size of the hula hoops.
- Provide a coach (not in a hoop) to direct each group.

To increase the challenge:

- Permit only one person in a hoop at a time.
- Increase the number of participants in each group.
- Reduce the size of the hoops.
- Use a stopwatch to record the time it takes the group members to reverse their positions.

Self-Check Questions

- Am I communicating well with my group?
- Am I showing respect for my group mates?
- Am I applying critical thinking skills to help my group solve problems?

SUPPORT SIGNALS

Activity Goal

To communicate with a partner without speaking.

Fundamental Movement Skills

Running, skipping, hopping

Tactical Focus

- Demonstrate behaviors that help a partner feel physically and emotionally safe while traveling backward.
- Demonstrate communication skills while working collaboratively with a partner.

Level

Competent

Facility

Gymnasium or outdoors

Equipment

None

Time

15 to 20 minutes

Activity Category

Cooperative games

Safety

Ensure that indoor and outdoor activity spaces are a safe distance from walls and free of hazards (e.g., benches, equipment, basketball nets, holes, loose gravel, wet grass); remove or mark any hazards. Provide safe distances between pairs working in the same space. Remind participants to keep their heads up and to be aware of others when moving through the space.

Activity Instructions

Participants work in pairs. Without speaking, partners move—one backward and one forward. Partners begin by walking and, as appropriate, progress to skipping, galloping, and possibly jogging. Encourage partners to create signals to communicate with each other as they move. Change leaders often.

Adaptations

To decrease the challenge:

- Have participants hold hands while moving.
- Have all participants move in the same direction around the activity space.
- Allow participants to speak a few words decided on by the whole group.

To increase the challenge:

- Increase the level of intensity of the assigned movement.
- Have participants travel through an obstacle course (e.g., around hula hoops, over benches).

Self-Check Questions

- Am I communicating well with my partner?
- Am I showing respect for my partner and working within his comfort zone?
- Do my actions help my partner feel safe?

WHAT'S THE WI-FI PASSWORD?

Activity Goal

To work cooperatively with teammates to decipher the correct order of cones.

Fundamental Movement Skill

Running

Tactical Focus

- Demonstrate critical thinking skills while working collaboratively in a group to guess the password.
- Demonstrate movement skills safely while traveling in the activity area.

Level

Competent

Facility

Gymnasium or outdoors

Equipment

4 groups of 8 cones

Time

15 to 20 minutes

Activity Category

Cooperative games

Safety

Ensure that indoor and outdoor activity spaces are a safe distance from walls and free of hazards (e.g., benches, equipment, basketball nets, holes, loose gravel, wet grass); remove or mark any hazards. Provide safe distances between games occurring in the same space. Remind participants to keep their heads up and to be aware of others when moving through the space.

Activity Instructions

Prior to the activity, number four sets of cones from 1 to 8. Determine an order for the cones that participants will try to guess. All four groups will be trying to guess the same password.

Divide participants into four groups. Each group has eight cones that are placed at the opposite end of their activity space. One at a time, group members run to the cones and move only one cone to try to place them in the correct order to crack the Wi-Fi login code. After moving only one cone, each participant runs back to their team and tags the next teammate who will move a cone and try to hack the code. The returning hacker chooses an on-the-spot physical activity for all group members to perform (e.g., jumping jack, squat, heel dig) while waiting for the next participants to return. Groups should work together to develop a strategy for completing the task as quickly as possible. Travel among the groups letting them know how many numbers they have in the correct order and eventually tell them which numbers are in the correct order.

Adaptations

To decrease the challenge

- Allow two group members to move cones at once.
- Decrease the size of the activity space.
- Reduce the number of cones per group.

To increase the challenge:

- Increase the number of cones per group.
- Do not allow group members to speak to each other.
- Increase the size of the activity space.

Self-Check Questions

- Am I communicating well with my group mates?
- Do I apply movement skills to travel safely in the activity area?
- Am I demonstrating critical thinking skills to help my group guess the password?

Activity Goal

To be the first to respond to the "Look" command.

Fundamental Movement Skill

Coordination

Tactical Focus

- Demonstrate safe movement skills while performing an optimal challenge.
- Apply strategies to respond quickly to the group.

Level

Proficient

Facility

Gymnasium or outdoors

Equipment

None

Time

15 to 20 minutes

Activity Category

Individual pursuits

Safety

Ensure that indoor and outdoor activity spaces are a safe distance from walls and free of hazards (e.g., benches, equipment, basketball nets, holes, loose gravel, wet grass); remove or mark any hazards. Provide safe distances between circles. Remind participants to be aware of others in the space.

Activity Instructions:

Divide participants into two or three circles and have them perform a physical task (e.g., jogging, jumping jack, squat) while looking at their feet. When you call out "Look," participants quickly look directly across from them at another participant in the circle and call out "Don't look" attempting to be the first to look before the participant across from them. The participant who is the slowest at calling out "Don't look" moves to stand behind the winning participant. The winning participant determines the next task that they and the other participants in the circle will perform.

Adaptations

To decrease the challenge:

- Decrease the intensity of the physical tasks.
- Increase the number of participants in the circle.

To increase the challenge:

- Increase the intensity of the physical tasks.
- Call out "Look" more frequently.

Self-Check Questions

- Do I apply strategies to avoid making eye contact?
- Do I demonstrate controlled and safe movements?
- Do I demonstrate fair play by following the rules?

NUMBER SLIDER

Activity Goal

To work as a team to unscramble a number puzzle.

Fundamental Movement Skill

Running

Tactical Focus

- Demonstrate fair play by communicating with the team effectively and following the rules of the game.
- Apply problem-solving skills to support the team in developing successful strategies.
- Apply movement skills to travel safely in the activity area.

Level

Proficient

Facility

Gymnasium or outdoors

Equipment

7 cones per group, floor tape to create a 3- by 3-foot (1 by 1 m) grid containing 9 squares for each team

Time

15 to 20 minutes

Activity Category

Cooperative games

Safety

Ensure that indoor and outdoor activity spaces are a safe distance from walls and free of hazards (e.g., benches, equipment, basketball nets, holes, loose gravel, wet grass); remove or mark any hazards. Provide safe distances between games occurring in the same space. Remind participants to keep their heads up and to be aware of others when moving through the space.

Activity Instructions

Prior to the activity, number seven cones 1 through 7 for each team. Use floor tape to create a 3- by 3-foot (1 by 1 m) grid that contains nine squares for each team. Place the numbered cones in a random order on the grid with one cone per square; two squares will be empty.

Divide participants into teams of four or five. Each team has seven cones on its grid. Players line up at the opposite end of the activity area from the grid. On your signal (e.g., whistle, "Go"), one player from each team races to the team's grid and moves one cone to an open square to begin the process of placing the cones in order from 1 to 7. The first

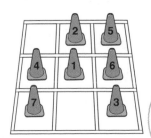

runner returns to the team and tags the next runner, who then moves the second cone. The returning player leads the waiting group in a physical task (e.g., jogging, jumping jack, squat). The game continues until all of the cones have been placed in order from 1 to 7. Encourage teams to communicate and strategize their moves.

Adaptations

To decrease the challenge:

- Allow two players to move cones at once.
- Decrease the distance between the grid and the runners' start line.
- Reduce the number of cones in the grid.

To increase the challenge:

- Do not allow teammates to talk to each other.
- Increase the distance between the grid and the runners' start line.
- Limit the number of moves players can make with the cones.

Self-Check Questions

- Do I demonstrate fair play by following the rules of the game?
- Do I think critically to support my team in developing strategies for success?
- Do I apply movement skills to travel safely in the activity area?

GROUP JUGGLE

Activity Goal

To work in a group to send and receive as many objects as possible.

Fundamental Movement Skills

Overhead volley, throwing underhand

Tactical Focus

- Demonstrate movement skills to consistently send and receive an object.
- Work collaboratively with a team to control an object.

Level

Proficient

Facility

Gymnasium or outdoors

Equipment

15 to 20 beach balls, volleyballs, balloons (various sizes and colors)

Time

15 to 20 minutes

Activity Category

Cooperative games

Safety

Ensure that indoor and outdoor activity spaces are a safe distance from walls and free of hazards (e.g., benches, equipment, basketball nets, holes, loose gravel, wet grass); remove or mark any hazards. Provide safe distances between circles. Remind participants to keep their heads up and to be aware of other groups in the space.

Activity Instructions

Divide participants into groups of four to six, and have each form a circle. Players strike (e.g., throw underhand, hit, volley, or bump) an object into the air and try not to let it touch the floor. Players cannot pass to the person beside them. Once players have control of the object, add a second one. Continue adding objects to determine the maximum number the group can control.

Adaptations

To decrease the challenge:

- Have participants send to the same people each time, forming a passing and receiving pattern.
- Have more players per group.
- Allow players to catch the object before throwing to a teammate.

To increase the challenge:

- Do not allow players to speak; however, they can make robot sounds (e.g., yip, pop, beep, boop) when receiving or sending (one sound per player).
- Require that players remain seated.
- Use smaller objects.

Self-Check Questions

- Am I communicating well with my group and demonstrating fair play?
- Am I using controlled force to send the object to my group mates?
- Do I demonstrate appropriate skills, techniques, and tactics to send and receive an object?

CHAPTER 2

Personal Fitness

This chapter focuses on four of the health-related components of fitness: cardio-respiratory fitness, muscular strength, muscular endurance, and flexibility. Participants explore a variety of games, stations, and challenges that provide opportunities to further develop their knowledge of these components and improve their personal fitness.

Words to Know

- **Cardiorespiratory fitness.** The ability of both the circulatory and respiratory systems to maintain aerobic activity for sustained periods of time.
- **Flexibility.** The ability to move the joints of the body through a full range of motion.
- **Muscular endurance.** The capacity of muscles to perform over a sustained period of time.
- **Muscular strength.** The total amount of force a muscle can produce.

Where's the Physical Literacy?

Personal fitness benefits the development of the whole person and supports people in creating habits or respect for both themselves and others. While focusing on the four components of health-related fitness, participants develop a deeper understanding of their personal fitness strengths and limitations. An analysis of their achievements through self-reflection and personal comparison can create the motivation and inspiration to move more. The activities in this chapter help participants use fundamental movement skills to develop confidence and competence.

Educator Check and Reflect

- Establish an emotionally safe learning environment.
- As participants' fitness levels improve, consider increasing the length of the activities.
- Encourage participants to assess their own levels of health-related fitness (e.g., reflect on strengths and areas in need of improvement, set goals, and develop personal fitness plans).
- Guide participants in focusing exclusively on self-awareness and self-monitoring and not on comparing themselves to others or established standards.
- Provide simple and noninvasive ways for participants to monitor their perceived exertion, such as the talk test (the ability to talk comfortably), the audible breath check (the ability to hear their own breath), and the breath rate test (analyzing the speed at which they are breathing).
- Because music is a great motivator, consider using music during activities and as starting and stopping signals. Choose music that has a strong beat and age-appropriate messages.

Activity Goal

To collect as many playing cards as possible while performing a variety of physical tasks.

Fundamental Movement Skill

Running

Tactical Focus

- Understand personal areas of strength and those needing improvement.
- Apply appropriate movement skills while moving safely throughout the activity space.

Level

Beginning

Facility

Gymnasium or outdoors

Equipment

1 deck of playing cards

Time

5 to 10 minutes

Activity Category

Individual pursuits

Safety

Ensure that indoor and outdoor activity spaces are a safe distance from walls and free of hazards (e.g., benches, equipment, basketball nets, holes, loose gravel, wet grass); remove or mark any hazards. Remind participants to keep their heads up and to be aware of others when moving through the space.

Activity Instructions

Prior to the start of the activity, work with participants to assign one physical task to each of the four suits in a card deck. Consider having all tasks focus on the same component of health-related fitness (e.g., to focus on flexibility: hearts = standing forward fold to touch toes, clubs = overhead side stretch, spades = hands on waist for gentle back bend, diamonds = low side lunge). Review the tasks and consider displaying them for reference.

Each participant receives one playing card. On your signal, participants run through the activity space exchanging cards with other participants. On a second signal, participants freeze and perform the task that corresponds to the suit of their card. On the next signal, participants return to exchanging cards, and the activity continues for a time period you have chosen.

Adaptations

To decrease the challenge:

- Decrease the intensity level of the tasks.
- Have participants form pairs and choose which of their two tasks to perform.
- Reduce the time participants spend performing the tasks.

To increase the challenge:

- Increase the intensity level of the tasks.
- Have the number value of the card indicate how many repetitions participants perform.
- Have participants track the number of repetitions they performed and try to beat that number each round.

Self-Check Questions

- Am I moving safely in relation to the other participants?
- Am I able to monitor how hard I am working throughout the task?
- Do I understand my own strengths when performing fitness activities?

Activity Goal

To spell several words while performing a variety of physical tasks.

Fundamental Movement Skills

Running, jumping, skipping

Tactical Focus

- Understand personal areas of strength and those needing improvement.
- Work collaboratively with a partner to spell words correctly.

Level

Beginning

Facility

Gymnasium or outdoors

Equipment

ABC fitness poster (see table 2.1)

Time

15 to 20 minutes

Activity Category

Individual pursuits

Safety

Ensure that indoor and outdoor activity spaces are a safe distance from walls and free of hazards (e.g., benches, equipment, basketball nets, holes, loose gravel, wet grass); remove or mark any hazards. Provide safe distances between activities occurring in the same space. Remind participants to keep their heads up and to be aware of others when moving through the space.

Activity Instructions

Prior to the activity, assign one physical task to each letter of the alphabet. Display tasks on a single poster or on 26 station cards scattered throughout the activity space. Table 2.1 shows possible tasks you might include.

Working in pairs, participants take turns spelling both of their names and performing the task assigned to each letter. Choose a repetition number or time requirement for each letter (e.g., 10 repetitions or 10 seconds). Consider reviewing unfamiliar movements at the beginning of the activity. If using stations, have participants move to each station using a variety of fundamental movement skills (e.g., run, jump, skip). In a school setting participants might also spell high-frequency words or word wall words from a recent topic of study.

Adaptations

To decrease the challenge:

- Decrease the intensity level of the tasks.
- Decrease the number of repetitions or the time spent on each task.
- Review and display a list of familiar words for participants to spell.
- Spell a word as a whole group so that participants understand letter tasks.
- Instead of doing the letter tasks, have participants choose one task (e.g., five jumping jacks) and perform the task at each letter as they spell a word as a group.

To increase the challenge:

- Increase the length and difficulty of words.
- Increase the number of repetitions or the time spent on each task.
- Assign a repetition number or time for each task based on its intensity.

Self-Check Questions

- Am I able to monitor how hard I am working throughout the task?
- Do I work collaboratively with my partner to spell words correctly?
- Can I recognize areas of fitness in which I need to improve?

Table 2.1 Possible Poster Activities for ABC Fitness

A = Alternating side leg swing. Standing tall, swing legs one at a time from side to side.	B = Boxing jog. Jog on the spot punching arms out in front or above the body.	C = Calf raise. Standing on toes, lift and lower the heels.	D = Downward-facing dog. On all fours, press the seat up, forming an upside-down V.	E = Energizer star jump. Jump, forming the letter X while in the air.
F = Flutter kick standing. Standing, kick the legs in front of the body as quickly as possible.	G = Gallop. Step forward with the front foot followed by the back foot; repeat with the same foot forward. Feet never cross or touch.	H = Head, shoulders, knees, and toes. Both hands touch the head, shoulders, knees, and toes five times fast.	I = Intense speed-skater. Hop from side to side while imitating a skating action.	J = Jumping jack. Standing with legs together and arms at sides, jump so the legs are wide apart and the arms are stretched overhead.
K = Knee raise. Jog or march in place lifting the knees as high as possible.	L = Lunge. Stepping forward with one foot, lower the body so both knees are bent to 90 degrees; repeat on the other side.	M = Mountain climbers. From a plank position with shoulders above wrists, march or jog the knees toward the chest.	N = Noisy steps. Stomp in place as loudly as possible.	O = Octopus arms. Jog in place wiggling the arms out from the sides of the body.
P = Plank. On hands or elbows and knees or toes, engage the core and form a straight line with the body.	Q = Quickly jog in place. Jog in place as fast as possible.	R = Rocking horse. From a standing position, rock forward and backward alternating lifting one knee toward the chest and curling the opposite foot backward toward the seat.	S = Squat. Standing with feet hip-distance apart, bend the knees to lower the body until the seat is aligned with the knees; return to standing.	T = Tuck jump. Jump hugging both knees toward the chest.
U = Up-and-down jump. Jump in place raising both arms above the head and then down toward the floor.	V = V-sit. Sitting on the floor, stretch both legs up with or without holding the backs of the knees, to form the letter V. Keep the chest lifted.	W = Walk like a bear. On all fours with knees lifted, crawl four steps forward and four steps backward.	X = X-jumps. Standing with legs and arms outstretched, jump crossing the arms in front of the body and crossing the legs.	Y = Yoga tree pose. Standing on one leg, bend the knee, placing the foot of the other leg on the ankle, calf, or thigh.
Z = Zigzag slide. Slide from side to side in a zigzag formation.				

FIT PUZZLE RELAY

Activity Goal

To collect puzzle pieces while performing a variety of physical tasks.

Fundamental Movement Skill

Running

Tactical Focus

- Communicate effectively as a group.
- Understand personal areas of strength and those needing improvement.
- Work at an optimal challenge level by using personal tactics (e.g., setting personal goals, counting repetitions or time out loud, monitoring perceived exertion and breath rate).

Level

Beginning

Facility

Gymnasium or outdoors

Equipment

4 to 6 puzzles with 10 to 12 pieces each

Time

10 to 15 minutes

Activity Category

Individual pursuits

Safety

Ensure that indoor and outdoor activity spaces are a safe distance from walls and free of hazards (e.g., benches, equipment, basketball nets, holes, loose gravel, wet grass); remove or mark any hazards. Provide safe distances between teams. Remind participants to keep their heads up and to be aware of others when moving through the space.

Activity Instructions

Prior to the start of the activity, assign one physical task (e.g., jumping jack, squat, running in place) to each puzzle piece for all puzzles. Write one task on the back of each puzzle piece. Consider using different color markers for each puzzle to keep the pieces organized. Review the tasks with the participants prior to starting the activity.

Have participants form groups of four to six and stand single file at one end of the activity space. Place each group's assigned puzzle at the opposite end of the space. One participant from each group runs to the group's puzzle, selects one piece, and returns it to the group. Participants then perform the physical task written on the back of the puzzle piece while the next participant races to collect another piece. Once all of the team's pieces have been collected, participants quickly and cooperatively put the puzzle together.

Adaptations

To decrease the challenge:

- Decrease the intensity level of the physical tasks.
- Reduce the distance between the groups and the puzzles.
- Have participants perform familiar movements.

To increase the challenge:

- Increase the intensity level of the physical tasks.
- Have each participant perform a different type of movement when retrieving a puzzle piece (e.g., lunge across the gym, jump squat).
- Increase the number of pieces in the puzzle.

Self-Check Questions

- Am I speaking nicely with those in my group?
- Do I know which fitness activities I am good at?
- Can I recognize areas of fitness in which I need to improve?

SUITS

Activity Goal

To collect as many playing cards as possible while performing a variety of physical tasks.

Fundamental Movement Skills

Running, jumping, skipping

Tactical Focus

- Understand personal areas of strength and those needing improvement.
- Work at an optimal challenge level by using personal tactics (e.g., setting personal goals, counting repetitions or time out loud, monitoring perceived exertion and breath rate).

Level

Exploring

Facility

Gymnasium or outdoors

Equipment

2 or 3 decks of playing cards

Time

10 to 15 minutes

Activity Category

Individual pursuits

Safety

Ensure that indoor and outdoor activity spaces are a safe distance from walls and free of hazards (e.g., benches, equipment, basketball nets, holes, loose gravel, wet grass); remove or mark any hazards. Provide safe distances between groups. Remind participants to keep their heads up and to be aware of others when moving through the space.

Activity Instructions

Prior to the start of the activity, work with participants to assign one physical task to each of the four suits in a card deck. Consider having all tasks focus on the same component of health-related fitness (e.g., to focus on cardiorespiratory fitness: hearts = jogging in place, clubs = jumping jack, spades = cross-country ski hop, diamonds = jumping lunge). Review the tasks and consider displaying them for reference.

Participants form groups of four or five. With all of the playing cards in a central area, groups circle the cards, each forming a single-file line an equal distance from the deck. On your signal, the first participant in each line runs to the deck, selects one card, returns it to the group, and moves to the end of the line. The group performs the task indicated by the card's suit as the next person in line races to select a second card from the deck. Consider having participants use a variety of fundamental movement skills when moving to retrieve a card (e.g., run, jump, skip). The race continues until no cards remain, or until an appropriate time. Consider having participants count their cards or add the numerical value of each card (face cards represent 10).

Adaptations

To decrease the challenge:

- Decrease the intensity level of the physical tasks.
- Reduce the distance between the groups and the cards.
- Display photographs or pictures illustrating how the tasks are performed.

To increase the challenge:

- Increase the intensity level of the physical tasks.
- Increase the distance between the groups and the cards.
- Have the number value of the card indicate how many repetitions of the task to perform.

Self-Check Questions

- Can I monitor how hard I am working throughout the task?
- Do I understand my own strengths when performing fitness tasks?
- Can I recognize areas of fitness in which I need to improve?

YOGA ZOO

Activity Goal

To move creatively while performing a variety of physical tasks.

Fundamental Movement Skill

Balance

Tactical Focus

- Understand personal areas of strength and those needing improvement.
- Work collaboratively with a partner.

Level

Exploring

Facility

Gymnasium or outdoors

Equipment

Index cards, writing utensils, mats (yoga or folding) (per participant)

Time

15 to 20 minutes

Activity Category

Individual pursuits

Safety

Ensure that indoor and outdoor activity spaces are a safe distance from walls and free of hazards (e.g., benches, equipment, basketball nets, holes, loose gravel, wet grass); remove or mark any hazards. Provide safe distances between groups. Remind participants to keep their heads up and to be aware of others when moving through the space.

Activity Instructions

Review with participants common animal-themed yoga poses (e.g., downward-facing dog, upward-facing dog, cat, cobra, cow, eagle). Be sure to highlight safety considerations and tactics used to maintain balance. Each participant receives one index card and a writing utensil.

Participants write or draw one animal or pose on the card. This can be a traditional yoga pose or one they've made up.

Participants form groups of four to six and teach their animal poses to the others in the group. Groups select three poses they can perform well as a team and share them with the larger group. The participants watching try to guess the pose the group is performing before trying it on their own.

Adaptations

To decrease the challenge:

- Decrease the challenge level of the poses.
- Have participants use equipment, benches, or the wall to safely support their poses.
- Review an animal book with participants prior to the activity.

To increase the challenge:

- Decrease the number of body parts that touch the floor in the poses.
- Have participants close their eyes while holding their poses.
- Have participants create animal poses at high or low levels.

Self-Check Questions

- Am I moving safely in relation to the other participants?
- Am I able to monitor how hard I am working throughout the task?
- Do I understand my own strengths when performing fitness tasks?

RUN AND ROLL

Activity Goal

To complete as many physical tasks as possible during a partner's lap.

Fundamental Movement Skill

Running

Tactical Focus

- Communicate effectively with a partner.
- Understand personal areas of strength and those needing improvement.

- Work at an optimal challenge level by using personal tactics (e.g., setting personal goals, counting repetitions or time out loud, monitoring perceived exertion and breath rate).

Level
Exploring

Facility
Gymnasium or outdoors

Equipment
Poster of tasks, dice (1 per pair)

Time
10 to 15 minutes

Activity Category
Individual pursuits

Safety
Ensure that indoor and outdoor activity spaces are a safe distance from walls and free of hazards (e.g., benches, equipment, basketball nets, holes, loose gravel, wet grass); remove or mark any hazards. Provide safe distances between pairs. Remind participants to keep their heads up and to be aware of others when moving through the space.

Activity Instructions
Prior to the start of the activity, assign one physical task to each side of a die (e.g., 1 = jumping jack, 2 = squat, 3 = bell hop, 4 = skier jump, 5 = lunge, 6 = plank). Record these on a poster for reference. Review the tasks with participants.

Participants form pairs and stand together at one side of the activity space. Partners determine who is partner A and who is partner B. Partner A rolls a die and performs the assigned task, while partner B runs one lap of the gym. When partner B returns to the starting line, partner B rolls the die while partner A runs. Have partners continue until an appropriate finish time. If appropriate, challenge partners to keep track of the laps they were able to run during the designated time.

Adaptations
To decrease the challenge:

- Display photographs or pictures illustrating how the tasks are performed.
- Decrease the intensity of the physical tasks.
- Reduce the size of the running area.

To increase the challenge:

- Increase the intensity of the physical tasks.
- Challenge partners to try to complete the most laps within the group.
- Increase the size of the running area.

Self-Check Questions

- Am I able to monitor my perceived exertion (via breath rate, talk test, or heart rate) to ensure that I am working at my optimal challenge level?
- Do I understand my own strengths when performing fitness tasks?
- Can I recognize areas of fitness in which I need to improve?

LAPS

Activity Goal

To perform a variety of physical tasks while completing as many station rounds as possible.

Fundamental Movement Skills

Running, jumping, skipping

Tactical Focus

- Communicate effectively as a group.
- Understand personal areas of strength and those needing improvement.
- Work at an optimal challenge level by using personal tactics (e.g., setting personal goals, counting repetitions or time out loud, monitoring perceived exertion and breath rate).

Level

Exploring

Facility

Gymnasium or outdoors

Equipment

8 to 10 stations, 20 to 30 popsicle sticks

Time

15 to 20 minutes

Activity Category

Individual pursuits

Safety

Ensure that indoor and outdoor activity spaces are a safe distance from walls and free of hazards (e.g., benches, equipment, basketball nets, holes, loose gravel, wet grass); remove or mark any hazards. Provide safe distances between stations. Remind participants to keep their heads up and to be aware of others at stations and when moving between stations.

Activity Instructions

Prior to the start of the activity, work with participants to assign to each of 8 to 10 activity stations one physical task as well as the number of repetitions to complete. Consider having all activities focus on the same component of health-related fitness (e.g., to focus on cardiorespiratory endurance, include jumping jack, high-knee jog, cross-country skier hop, bell hop, heel dig, shuttle run, skipping, skater hop). Review the activities for form and safety. Place stations a safe distance from each other throughout the activity space.

Divide participants into 8 to 10 groups. Each group selects a starting station and, on your signal, performs the task. Once all members have finished the task, the group travels together to the next station. Groups receive a popsicle stick each time they make it through all the stations. They continue for as many rounds as possible trying to collect the most popsicle sticks during the activity time.

Adaptations

To decrease the challenge:

- Display photographs or pictures illustrating how the station tasks are performed.
- Decrease the intensity of the physical tasks.
- Reduce the number of repetitions to complete at each station.

To increase the challenge:

- Increase the intensity of the physical tasks.
- Have participants keep track of their perceived exertion (via breath rate or heart rate) at each station.
- Consider including equipment (e.g., skipping ropes or stability balls), if available.

Self-Check Questions

- Am I able to monitor how hard I am working throughout the task?
- Do I understand my own strengths when performing fitness tasks?
- Can I recognize areas of fitness in which I need to improve?

DOUBLE DICE FITNESS STATIONS

Activity Goal

To perform a variety of physical tasks while moving through fitness stations.

Fundamental Movement Skill

Running

Tactical Focus

- Understand personal areas of strength and those needing improvement.
- Work at an optimal challenge level by using personal tactics (e.g., setting personal goals, counting repetitions or time out loud, monitoring perceived exertion and breath rate).

Level

Competent

Facility

Gymnasium or outdoors

Time

15 to 20 minutes

Equipment

8 to 10 station cards, 16 to 20 dice (two per station)

Activity Category

Individual pursuits

Safety

Ensure that indoor and outdoor activity spaces are a safe distance from walls and free of hazards (e.g., benches, equipment, basketball nets, holes, loose gravel, wet grass); remove or mark any hazards. Provide safe distances between stations. Remind participants to keep their heads up and to be aware of others at stations and when moving between stations.

Activity Instructions

Prior to the start of the activity, work with participants to assign one physical task to each of 8 to 10 activity stations. Consider having all activities focus on the same component of health-related fitness (e.g., a focus on muscular endurance might include squat, lunge, push-up, triceps dip, wall sit, plank, side plank, and single-leg deadlift). Review the activities for form and safety. Display stations a safe distance from each other throughout the activity space. Place two dice at each station.

Divide participants into 8 to 10 groups, and have each group select a starting station. Group members review the station card and then roll both dice to determine how many repetitions of the task to perform (for the plank and side plank, they hold the position for the given number of seconds). Participants make their way through each of the stations until all stations have been completed or they come to a stop at an appropriate finish time.

Adaptations

To decrease the challenge:

- Display photographs or pictures illustrating how the tasks are performed.
- Decrease the intensity of the physical tasks.
- Use only one die.
- When participants are working at the stations for the first time, don't use any dice.

To increase the challenge:

- Increase the intensity of the physical tasks.
- Have participants keep track of their perceived exertion (via breath rate or heart rate) at each station.

- Consider including equipment (e.g., skipping ropes or stability balls), if available.

Self-Check Questions
- Am I able to monitor how hard I am working throughout the tasks?
- Do I understand my own strengths when performing fitness tasks?
- Can I recognize areas of fitness in which I need to improve?

CARDIO UP CHALLENGE

Activity Goal
To complete a variety of participant-identified cardiorespiratory challenges.

Fundamental Movement Skills
Running, jumping, skipping

Tactical Focus
- Communicate effectively as a group.
- Understand personal areas of strength and those needing improvement.
- Work at an optimal challenge level by using personal tactics (e.g., setting personal goals, counting repetitions or time out loud, monitoring perceived exertion and breath rate).

Level
Competent

Facility
Gymnasium or outdoors

Equipment
Poster paper, marker

Time
20 to 25 minutes

Activity Category

Individual pursuits

Safety

Ensure that indoor and outdoor activity spaces are a safe distance from walls and free of hazards (e.g., benches, equipment, basketball nets, holes, loose gravel, wet grass); remove or mark any hazards. Provide safe distances between activities occurring in the same space. Remind participants to keep their heads up and to be aware of others when moving through the space.

Activity Instructions

Prior to the start of the activity, work with participants to create 8 to 10 cardiorespiratory challenges. Record the challenges on poster paper for reference.

Participants form groups of four or five in which they work together to complete all of the fitness challenges identified on the poster paper. Groups can perform the challenges in any order, but members must work together until every participant has completed them.

Suggested cardiorespiratory challenges:

- Perform five jumping jacks in each corner.
- Skip, touching three walls.
- High-five four people who are wearing your school colors.
- Complete 10 mountain climbers by each doorway.
- Run around the activity space twice.
- Complete 20 jumping lunges anywhere in the activity space.
- Hold plank in the center of the activity space while singing "Happy Birthday."
- Perform five push-ups near the equipment room.
- Perform grapevine one length of the gym.
- Perform five skater hops under each basketball net.

Adaptations

To decrease the challenge:

- Reduce the number of tasks.
- Decrease the intensity of the tasks.
- Provide 12 suggested tasks and allow participants to choose 8.
- Have participants work in pairs.

- Ask all participants to rate each cardio challenge as a star or stair. Star challenges are easy; stair challenges are those they need to practice. Have participants start with star challenges.

To increase the challenge:

- Increase the intensity of the tasks.
- Set a time limit in which groups must complete the tasks.
- Require participants to perform additional cardiorespiratory activities between missions (e.g., 25 jumping jacks).

Self-Check Questions

- Do I communicate well with my group mates?
- Am I moving safely in relation to the other participants?
- Can I recognize areas of fitness in which I need to improve?

ROCK-PAPER-SCISSORS ROTATION

Activity Goal

To challenge partners to a game of full-body rock-paper-scissors and to perform a variety of tasks related to the components of health-related fitness.

Fundamental Movement Skill

Coordination

Tactical Focus

- Understand personal areas of strength and those needing improvement.
- Work at an optimal challenge level by using personal tactics (e.g., setting personal goals, counting repetitions or time out loud, monitoring perceived exertion and breath rate).

Level

Competent

Facility

Gymnasium or outdoors

Equipment

Poster paper, marker

Time

15 to 20 minutes

Activity Category

Individual pursuits

Safety

Ensure that indoor and outdoor activity spaces are a safe distance from walls and free of hazards (e.g., benches, equipment, basketball nets, holes, loose gravel, wet grass); remove or mark any hazards. Remind participants to keep their heads up and to be aware of others in the circle.

Activity Instructions

Working with a partner, all pairs form a circle. Partners challenge each other to a full-body version of the hand game rock-paper-scissors.
 Positions for full-body rock-paper-scissors:

- Rock: Crouch into a ball. Rock beats scissors.
- Paper: Stand with arms and legs spread out wide. Paper beats rock.
- Scissors: Stand in a lunge with both arms reaching forward. Scissors beats paper.

Practice a few rounds to ensure that everyone understands the game. Next identify three on-the-spot movements and the number of repetitions per movement and display them on poster paper for participant reference throughout the game. The winning participant decides which of the three on-the-spot movements the pairs complete and for how many repetitions. After three rounds, one partner in each pair moves clockwise around the circle to line up with a new partner, and the game is repeated.

Adaptations

To decrease the challenge:

- Decrease the intensity of the on-the-spot movements.
- Have participants call out loud "1, 2, 3, show" to share their moves at the same time.
- Display photographs or pictures illustrating how the two on-the-spot movements are performed.

To increase the challenge:

- Increase the intensity of the on-the-spot movements.
- Set a time limit in which pairs must complete their games.
- Require both partners to run to touch a wall before returning to the game.

Self-Check Questions

- Do I communicate well with my partner?
- Am I able to monitor how hard I am working throughout the task?
- Can I recognize areas of fitness in which I need to improve?

CRAZY CARD RELAY

Activity Goal

To perform a variety of physical tasks while waiting for a turn to run a lap.

Fundamental Movement Skill

Running

Tactical Focus

- Communicate effectively as a team.
- Understand personal areas of strength and those needing improvement.
- Work at an optimal challenge level by using personal tactics (e.g., setting personal goals, counting repetitions or time out loud, monitoring perceived exertion and breath rate).

Level

Competent

Facility

Gymnasium or outdoors

Equipment

Poster paper, marker, 1 deck of cards

Time

10 to 15 minutes

Activity Category

Individual pursuits

Safety

Ensure that indoor and outdoor activity spaces are a safe distance from walls and free of hazards (e.g., benches, equipment, basketball nets, holes, loose gravel, wet grass); remove or mark any hazards. Provide safe distances between teams. Remind participants to keep their heads up and to be aware of others when moving through the space.

Activity Instructions

Prior to the start of the activity, assign one physical task to each of the four suits of a deck of cards (e.g., hearts = jumping jack, clubs = squat, spades = bell hop, diamonds = plank). Review the activities with participants and consider recording them on poster paper.

Participants form teams of four and stand together at one side of the activity space. Teammates number themselves as first, second, third, and fourth runners. Each first runner lines up at the starting line and runs one lap of the activity area. One card from the deck is selected by one of the remaining three participants and they perform the corresponding physical task. The returning first runner tags the second runner, who runs, and the remaining teammates select a new card to determine the task to perform. The activity concludes when each runner has completed five laps or at an appropriate finish time.

Adaptations

To decrease the challenge:

- Display photographs or pictures illustrating how the tasks are performed.
- Decrease the intensity of the tasks.
- Reduce the size of the running area.

To increase the challenge:

- Increase the intensity of the tasks.
- Challenge teams to try to complete the most laps within the group.
- Increase the size of the running area.
- Have participants use different ways to travel around the activity space (e.g. skipping, jumping, galloping).

Self-Check Questions

- Am I able to monitor my perceived exertion (via breath rate, talk test, or heart rate) to ensure that I am working at my optimal challenge level?
- Do I understand my own strengths when performing fitness tasks?
- Can I recognize areas of fitness in which I need to improve?

LINE RACE

Activity Goal

To perform a variety of physical tasks while moving in a line through the activity space.

Fundamental Movement Skill

Coordination

Tactical Focus

- Communicate effectively as a group.
- Work at an optimal challenge level by using personal tactics (e.g., setting personal goals, counting repetitions or time out loud, monitoring perceived exertion and breath rate).

Level

Proficient

Facility

Gymnasium or outdoors

Equipment

None

Time

10 to 15 minutes

Activity Category

Individual pursuits

Safety

Ensure that indoor and outdoor activity spaces are a safe distance from walls and free of hazards (e.g., benches, equipment, basketball nets, holes, loose gravel, wet grass); remove or mark any hazards. Provide safe distances between groups. Remind participants to keep their heads up and to be aware of others when moving through the space.

Activity Instructions

Participants form groups of four or five and stand single file at one end of the activity space. The participant at the back of each line runs to the front of the line and leads the group in a physical task (e.g., squat, jumping jack, lunge). The new participant at the back races to the front and leads a second exercise copied by the group. The lines move slowly forward as each new leader races to the front of the line. The activity concludes when each group has made it to the end of the space or after an appropriate amount of time.

Adaptations

To decrease the challenge:

- Decrease the intensity of the tasks.
- Reduce the distance the lines must travel.
- Review and display a list of movements for participants to choose from.

To increase the challenge:

- Increase the intensity of the tasks.
- Do not allow leaders to repeat tasks.
- Set a time limit in which groups must complete the tasks.

Self-Check Questions

- Do I communicate well with my group mates?
- Am I able to monitor how hard I am working throughout the task?
- Can I recognize areas of fitness in which I need to improve?

Activity Goal

To work through stations related to the four components of health-related fitness.

Fundamental Movement Skills

Running, jumping, skipping, coordination

Tactical Focus

- Communicate effectively as a group.
- Understand personal areas of strength and those needing improvement.
- Work at an optimal challenge level by using personal tactics (e.g., setting personal goals, counting repetitions or time out loud, monitoring perceived exertion and breath rate).

Level

Proficient

Facility

Gymnasium or outdoors

Equipment

Station cards (letter-size paper), markers

Time

20 to 25 minutes

Activity Category

Individual pursuits

Safety

Ensure that indoor and outdoor activity spaces are a safe distance from walls and free of hazards (e.g., benches, equipment, basketball nets, holes, loose gravel, wet grass); remove or mark any hazards. Provide safe distances between stations. Remind participants to keep their heads up and to be aware of others when moving through the space.

Activity Instructions

Prior to the activity, participants divide into four groups. Assign each group one of the four components of health-related fitness, and have group members identify four moves for their component and write them in the corners of their station card. Review their choices before displaying the station cards in each corner of the activity area.

In their groups, participants move (e.g., run, hop, skip) among all four stations four times. Participants remain at each station for a designated amount of time (e.g., 45 to 60 seconds) performing the moves and rotate to the next station on your signal.

Adaptations

To decrease the challenge:

- Review a variety of movements for each component prior to the activity.
- Decrease the intensity of the tasks.
- Reduce the time spent at each station.

To increase the challenge:

- Increase the intensity of the tasks.
- Increase the time spent at each station.

Self-Check Questions

- Do I communicate well with my group mates?
- Am I able to monitor how hard I am working throughout the tasks?
- Can I recognize areas of fitness in which I need to improve?

ROCK-PAPER-SCISSORS BASEBALL

Activity Goal

To cross the home base as many times as possible, while playing full-body rock-paper-scissors.

Fundamental Movement Skills

Running, skipping, coordination

Tactical Focus

- Understand personal areas of strength and those needing improvement.

- Work at an optimal challenge level by using personal tactics (e.g., setting personal goals, counting repetitions or time out loud, monitoring perceived exertion and breath rate).

Level
Proficient

Facility
Gymnasium or outdoors

Equipment
None

Time
15 to 20 minutes

Activity Category
Individual pursuits

Safety
Ensure that indoor and outdoor activity spaces are a safe distance from walls and free of hazards (e.g., benches, equipment, basketball nets, holes, loose gravel, wet grass); remove or mark any hazards. Remind participants to keep their heads up and be aware of others when moving through the space.

Activity Instructions
Divide the activity area into four base areas, similar to baseball. Review the positions of full-body rock-paper-scissors:

- Rock: Crouch into a ball. Rock beats scissors.
- Paper: Stand with arms and legs spread out wide. Paper beats rock.
- Scissors: Stand in a lunge with both arms reaching forward. Scissors beats paper.

Have participants practice a few rounds to ensure that they understand the game. All participants begin at home base where they pair up to play a game of full-body rock-paper-scissors. The winning participants move (e.g., run, skip) to first base; those remaining find other partners to compete with. At second and third base, the game continues; winning participants move on and remaining participants find someone new to play with. Participants keep track of the number of times they pass home base. The game concludes after an appropriate amount of time.

Adaptations

To decrease the challenge:

- After two losses in a row, participants move to the next base.
- Have participants call out loud "1, 2, 3, show" to share their moves at the same time.

To increase the challenge:

- Set a time limit in which to complete a number of home runs.
- Have losing participants move back a base (e.g., from second base back to first base).

Self-Check Questions

- Do I communicate well with my partner?
- Am I able to monitor how hard I am working throughout the task?

DICE RELAY

Activity Goal

To perform a variety of physical tasks while completing a relay race.

Fundamental Movement Skill

Running

Tactical Focus

- Communicate effectively as a group.
- Understand personal areas of strength and those needing improvement.
- Work at an optimal challenge level by using personal tactics (e.g., setting personal goals, counting repetitions or time out loud, monitoring perceived exertion and breath rate).

Level

Proficient

Facility

Gymnasium or outdoors

Equipment

5 or 6 dice, marker, poster paper

Time

10 to 15 minutes

Activity Category

Individual pursuits

Safety

Ensure that indoor and outdoor activity spaces are a safe distance from walls and free of hazards (e.g., benches, equipment, basketball nets, holes, loose gravel, wet grass); remove or mark any hazards. Provide safe distances between groups. Remind participants to keep their heads up and to be aware of others when moving through the space.

Activity Instructions

Prior to the start of the activity, all participants work together to assign one physical task to each side of a die. Consider having all tasks focus on one health-related component of fitness (e.g., for cardiorespiratory fitness: 1 = jumping jack, 2 = mountain climber, 3 = bell hop, 4 = skier jump, 5 = jumping lunge, 6 = skater hop). Record participant choices on poster paper for reference.

Participants form groups of four or five and stand single file at one end of the gym. The first participant races to the opposite end of the gym, rolls a die, and calls out the number and corresponding task. All participants in the group perform the task. The runner then high-fives the next participant in line, who races to the die while the first runner moves to the back of the line. Participants continue performing the task until the runner calls out the next number and task. Participants continue until all group members have had a turn or until an appropriate amount of time has passed.

Adaptations

To decrease the challenge:

- Display photographs or pictures illustrating how the tasks are performed.
- Decrease the intensity of the tasks.
- Decrease the size of the running area.

To increase the challenge:

- Increase the intensity of the tasks.
- Increase the size of the running area.

Self-Check Questions

- Do I communicate well with my group mates?
- Am I able to monitor how hard I am working throughout the task?
- Can I recognize areas of fitness in which I need to improve?

CHAPTER 3

Gymnastics

This chapter emphasizes the fundamental movement skills of dynamic and static balance, jumping and landing, and running and skipping, as well as other locomotor movement skills (e.g., rolling and turning), movement concepts (e.g., body, space, effort, and relationships), and movement principles (e.g., center of gravity and laws of motion). These skills are explored alone, in pairs, or in small groups, and when moving on and off equipment (e.g., a bench). Safety is emphasized, as is self-monitoring within personal and shared activity spaces, and when moving on and off equipment.

Words to Know

- **Static balance.** The capacity to maintain a desired shape without movement while in a stationary position (e.g., V-sit, stork stand, T-scale).
- **Dynamic balance.** The ability to use core strength to maintain balance and body control while moving through space (e.g., turning, rolling, balancing, landing from a jump).
- **Jumping and landing.** The act of moving off a surface and into the air using both feet and then returning to the surface. A jump includes three phases: takeoff (preparation), flight (execution), and landing (follow-through).
- **Rotation.** Moving the body by turning around an axis or center.

Balance Transferable Skills

Balance
1. Focus on a stationary object (e.g., a point on the wall or floor).
2. Keep a tight body (e.g., maintain body control).
3. Keep body weight low and centered over the base of support.

Balance learning cues: Maintain tight muscles, stay still, keep the eyes focused, be creative.

Jumping and Landing Transferable Skills

Preparation	Execution	Follow-Through
1. Bend the knees. 2. Swing the arms forward with appropriate force to help move the body forward and up.	Keep the body tight.	1. Bend the knees to absorb the landing. 2. Keep the feet shoulder-width apart. 3. Hold the arms out for balance. 4. Keep the head up.

Jumping and landing learning cues: Bend the knees, swing the arms back and forward, extend the legs and feet at takeoff, land softly.

Rotation Transferable Skills

Jump Turn

1. Bend the knees.
2. Stand tall, jump up, reach both arms above the head, and rotate halfway or all the way around.
3. Land safely, bending the knees.

Jump turn learning cues: Bend the knees, jump for height, stretch the arms above the head, maintain balance, land softly.

Forward Roll

1. Squat and tuck facing the mat in a tight ball position with knees hugged in toward the chest and feet together.
2. Place fingers on the mat pointed toward the end of the mat with elbows pointing out.
3. Tuck the chin toward the chest.
4. Lift the hips while straightening the legs and bending the arms to roll on the back of the shoulders.
5. Continue in a tucked formation throughout the roll; then reach forward while standing up, with feet together and body tight.

Forward roll learning cues: Tuck facing the mat, hug the knees in a tight ball, tuck the chin toward the chest, lift the hips, roll on the back of the shoulders, stay tucked throughout the roll, stand up with a tight body.

Where's The Physical Literacy?

Gymnastics is a unique and diverse foundational activity that leads to the development of movement skills, concepts, and principles and helps to set the groundwork for other sports and pursuits. Gymnastics provides an opportunity to explore physical challenges and movement opportunities often not experienced in traditional games and pursuits.

Through gymnastics, participants actively explore stability and loco-motor skills, as well as the movement concepts of body, space, effort, and relationships. They also learn to self-monitor as they work within their comfort zones and at their levels of optimal challenge in pairs, in groups, and with equipment. At an early age participants explore the concept of the center of gravity while working on balance alone, in pairs, and in small groups. When practicing jumping and landing safely on the floor and off equipment, they play with laws of motion such as maximal velocity.

Educator Check and Reflect

- Refer to your recreation center, school, or school board safety guidelines regarding gymnastics and movement activities. Some station activities might require constant visual supervision.
- Encourage participants to work within their own comfort levels when trying new skills.
- The activities in this chapter require minimal equipment. If your facility doesn't have a required piece of equipment, modify the activities using available and facility-approved resources.
- Prior to instructing jumping and landing, always review safe landing procedures, especially before jumping from equipment.
- When spotting participants, stand in front and slightly to the side of the equipment or movement space. You or another participant can hold the person's hand or arm to provide support for maintaining balance, guide the person along a piece of equipment, or help the person move backward, as appropriate.
- To support participants who are new to rolling, consider using an inclined mat or creating an incline by folding mats so they can build momentum; this makes rolling easier.

FLASH CARD BALANCE

Activity Goal
To hold a traditional static balance pose displayed on a flash card.

Fundamental Movement Skill
Balance

Tactical Focus
- Demonstrate appropriate movement skills (e.g., extending arms to the side to increase stability while balancing).
- Develop and apply appropriate strategies to maintain balance (e.g., engage the core, keep the eyes on a stationary point).

Level
Beginning

Facility

Gymnasium or outdoors

Equipment

10 to 15 index cards, mats (1 per participant)

Time

5 to 20 minutes

Activity Category

Individual pursuits

Safety

Participants should work within their personal limits and perform only poses that have been taught during instruction. Ensure that indoor and outdoor activity spaces are a safe distance from walls and free of hazards (e.g., benches, equipment, basketball nets, holes, loose gravel, wet grass); remove or mark any hazards. Provide safe distances between participants, and remind them to keep their heads up and to be aware of others when moving through the space.

Activity Instructions

Prior to the start of the activity, use index cards to create a set of flash cards displaying traditional static balance poses (e.g., stork, T-scale, V-sit).

Participants scatter throughout the activity space, standing a safe distance from each other. As you hold up a flash card, participants imitate the static balance pose displayed on the card. Encourage them to hold the position for at least three seconds. Repeat with 10 to 15 cards as appropriate for participants.

Next, have participants move through the activity space in a variety of ways (e.g., skip, hop, gallop, slide). On your signal, participants freeze, you display a card, and they imitate the balance pose on the card. On the next signal, participants move again through the activity space.

Adaptations

To decrease the challenge:

- Have participants balance on more body parts at once.
- Allow participants to hold on to a wall or a secured chair to help them balance.

- Increase the amount of time participants spend focusing on one pose.
- Provide equipment participants can use to help them balance (e.g., hockey stick, chair, partner).

To increase the challenge:

- Have participants balance on fewer body parts at once.
- Ask participants to demonstrate how to change four-point poses to three-point poses.
- Require that participants close one or both eyes while holding their balance.
- Have participants balance on the same number of body parts, but with a partner.

Self-Check Questions

- Am I moving safely in relation to the other participants?
- Do I focus on an object or the wall to help me balance?
- Do I keep my body weight centered over my base of support?
- Can I modify the pose to make it easier or harder?

DICE ROLL BALANCE

Activity Goal

To hold a static balance pose on the number of body parts identified on a die.

Fundamental Movement Skill

Balance

Tactical Focus

- Demonstrate appropriate movement skills (e.g., extending arms to the side to increase stability while balancing).
- Develop and apply appropriate strategies to maintain balance (e.g., engage the core, keep the eyes on a stationary point).

Level

Beginning

Facility

Gymnasium or outdoors

Equipment

4 to 6 dice, mats (1 per participant)

Time

15 to 20 minutes

Activity Category

Individual pursuits

Safety

Participants should work within their personal limits and perform only balance poses that have been taught during instruction. Ensure that indoor and outdoor activity spaces are a safe distance from walls and free of hazards (e.g., benches, equipment, basketball nets, holes, loose gravel, wet grass); remove or mark any hazards. Provide safe distances between groups. Remind participants to keep their heads up and to be aware of others around them.

Activity Instructions

Participants form groups of four or five. Each group receives one die. Participants take turns rolling the die and performing unique static balance poses using the number of body parts identified by the number on the die (e.g., a rolled number 2 would require balancing on two body parts). Encourage them to hold the position for at least three seconds. Consider having groups that create unique balances demonstrate them for the entire group and have everyone imitate them.

Adaptations

To decrease the challenge:

- Allow participants to roll the die two or three times per turn and choose among the choices.
- Permit participants to hold on to a wall, a secured chair, or a partner to help them balance.
- Increase the amount of time participants spend focusing on one pose.

To increase the challenge:

- Add physical tasks for participants to perform between rolls (e.g., jumping jack, squat, jogging in place).

- Require that participants close one or both eyes while holding their balance poses.
- Have participants balance on the same number of body parts, but with a partner.
- Give each participant a beanbag that they must balance on a body part while balancing.

Self-Check Questions
- Am I moving safely in relation to the other participants?
- Am I in control of all of my body parts?
- Do I keep my body weight centered over my base of support?

BALANCE TAG

Activity Goal
To hold a static balance pose while playing a game of tag.

Fundamental Movement Skills
Agility, balance, running

Tactical Focus
- Demonstrate appropriate movement skills (e.g., extending arms to the side to increase stability while balancing).
- Develop and apply appropriate strategies to maintain balance (e.g., engage the core, keep the eyes on a stationary point).
- Develop and apply appropriate strategies to avoid being tagged (e.g., know who and where the taggers are, move quickly through the activity space).

Level
Beginning

Facility
Gymnasium or outdoors

Equipment
3 or 4 hula hoops (optional)

Time
15 to 20 minutes

Activity Category
Individual pursuits

Safety
Participants should work within their personal limits and perform only balance poses that have been taught during instruction. Ensure that indoor and outdoor activity spaces are a safe distance from walls and free of hazards (e.g., benches, equipment, basketball nets, holes, loose gravel, wet grass); remove or mark any hazards. Remind participants to keep their heads up and to be aware of others when moving through the space.

Activity Instructions
Invite two or three participants to volunteer to be taggers. The remaining participants scatter throughout the activity area. On your signal, participants move around the activity space in a variety of ways (e.g., run, skip, gallop, hop) trying to avoid being tagged. Participants are safe from being tagged when they hold a static balance pose. Consider showing pictures of poses that participants must mirror to avoid being tagged; review these prior to the activity. When tagged, players become taggers. Change taggers often. Consider scattering three or four hula hoops around the activity space to be safe areas in which to perform poses. If all hoops are occupied, participants must remain in the tag game.

Adaptations
To decrease the challenge:
- Let participants select their own locomotor skills.
- Allow participants to hold on to a wall or a secured chair to help them balance.
- Set a time limit for being taggers.
- Let participants choose easy balance poses.

To increase the challenge:
- Increase the difficulty of the balance poses.
- Reduce the size of the activity space.

- Increase the number of taggers.
- Require that tagged players perform a specific pose. To free a tagged player, another player must mirror the pose while both players count to 5.

Self-Check Questions

- Am I moving safely in relation to the other participants?
- Am I in control of all of my body parts?
- Do I use appropriate strategies to avoid being tagged?

ROCK AND ROLL

Activity Goal

To explore body positions while performing simple rolls.

Fundamental Movement Skill

Coordination

Tactical Focus

- Demonstrate movement skills appropriate for a roll.
- Develop and apply appropriate rolling strategies (e.g., keep chin tucked, bend arms and legs as appropriate and at appropriate times).
- Move safely while rolling.

Level

Beginning

Facility

Gymnasium or outdoors

Equipment

Mats (1 per participant), 4 rock and roll activity cards

Time

20 to 25 minutes

Activity Category

Individual pursuits

Safety

Participants should work within their personal limits and perform only rolls that have been taught during instruction. Ensure that indoor and outdoor activity spaces are a safe distance from walls and free of hazards (e.g., benches, equipment, basketball nets, holes, loose gravel, wet grass); remove or mark any hazards. Provide safe distances between groups. Remind participants to keep their heads up and to be aware of others when practicing rolls.

Activity Instructions

Working in small groups, participants explore each of the four rock and roll activities at the group's pace. Group members can then create a sequence of rolls with balance poses between them and a beginning and ending pose.

Rock and Roll Activity Cards

- Card 1: Log roll. Lie on the mat with your arms stretched out over your head. Keep your body straight and tightly activated through your core. Use your entire body to turn as you roll down the mat.
- Card 2: Egg roll. Facing sideways on the mat, squat and tuck in a tight ball position with your knees hugged in toward your chest. Lower yourself sideways over your knees onto your shoulder; then onto your back and over to your other shoulder to return to a low squat, tucked in a tight ball position on your feet.
- Card 3: Pencil roll. Lie on the mat with your arms by your sides. Keep your body straight, long, and tight. Use your entire body to turn as you roll down the mat.
- Card 4: Front roll. Squat and tuck facing the mat in a tight ball position with your knees hugged in toward your chest and your feet together. Place your fingers on the mat pointed toward the end of the mat with elbows pointing out. Tuck your chin toward your chest. Lift your hips while straightening your legs, and bending your arms to roll on the back of your shoulders. Continue in a tucked formation throughout the entire roll; then reach forward with your arms as you stand up with your feet together and body tight.

Adaptations

To decrease the challenge:

- Let participants choose one roll to focus on.

Physical Literacy on the Move

- Provide visuals or videos of the rolls.
- Increase the time spent on each roll.
- Use chalk to draw where each foot goes on the mat during the roll.

To increase the challenge:

- Have participants perform more than one roll in a sequence.
- Increase the speed of the rolls.

Self-Check Questions

- Am I moving safely?
- Do I keep my chin tucked in while rolling?
- Do I demonstrate respectful behavior and appreciate differences in my group members' abilities?

BENCH BALANCE STATIONS

Activity Goal

To demonstrate both static and dynamic balance while moving on equipment.

Fundamental Movement Skill

Balance

Tactical Focus

- Demonstrate appropriate movement skills (e.g., extending arms to the side to increase stability while balancing).
- Develop and apply appropriate strategies to maintain balance (e.g., engage the core, keep the eyes on a stationary point).
- Move safely onto and off equipment.

Level

Exploring

Facility

Gymnasium

Equipment

7 benches, 10 to 20 folding mats, 15 to 20 beanbags

Time

30 to 35 minutes

Activity Category

Individual pursuits

Safety

Participants should work within their personal limits and perform only balance poses that have been taught during instruction. Place mats around the benches, and make sure the benches are stable and in good working order. Participants should always land on their feet and bend their knees when jumping off equipment. Be sure to follow administrative safety policy regarding equipment use. Provide safe distances between stations. Remind participants to keep their heads up and to be aware of others when moving through the space.

Activity Instructions

Prior to the activity, create seven gymnastics stations around the activity area with appropriate equipment (benches and mats). If available, consider using text and photographs to demonstrate the movements at each station.

Participants form groups of four or five. Review each station prior to beginning the activity. Determine how long participants should work at each station.

- Station 1: Walking forward on the bench
- Station 2: Walking backward on the bench
- Station 3: Walking sideways using a side step on the bench
- Station 4: Walking sideways using a crossover step on the bench
- Station 5: Stepping over beanbags while walking in a variety of ways on the bench
- Station 6: Walking on the bench with a beanbag balanced on the head
- Station 7: Balancing in a variety of static positions on the knees or seat on a bench

Adaptations

To decrease the challenge:

- Use a line on the floor instead of a bench.
- Allow participants to hold the hand of a partner who is standing on the floor.
- Increase the time spent at each station.

- Have one participant sit on the bench to hold it stable.

To increase the challenge:

- Require that participants change the movement while moving on the bench (e.g., slide, skip, hop).
- Have participants close one or both eyes while holding their balance on the bench.
- Have participants practice standing balance poses on one or more body parts.

Self-Check Questions

- Am I moving safely in relation to the equipment?
- Do I focus on a spot on the bench or the wall to help me balance?
- Do I keep my body weight centered over my base of support?

FOUR-CORNER PARTNER BALANCE

Activity Goal

To hold a static balance pose with a partner.

Fundamental Movement Skill

Balance

Tactical Focus

- Demonstrate appropriate movement skills while holding a static balance pose (e.g., extending arms to the side to increase stability, being aware of body position in relation to a partner).
- Develop and apply appropriate strategies to balance with a partner (e.g., engage the core, keep the eyes on a stationary point, communicate with a partner).
- Work collaboratively and communicate effectively with a partner.

Level

Exploring

Facility

Gymnasium

Equipment

4 partner balance formation signs, 20 to 25 mats

Time

10 to 15 minutes

Activity Category

Individual pursuits

Safety

Participants should work within their personal limits and perform only balance poses that have been taught during instruction. Ensure that indoor activity spaces are free of hazards (e.g., benches, equipment, basketball nets, poles); remove or mark any hazards. Provide safe distances between partners, and remind participants to keep their heads up and to be aware of others when moving through the space.

Activity Instructions

Prior to the activity, write the phrases *Front to front, Back to back, Front to back,* and *Side to side* on paper to display in each corner of the activity space.

Working in pairs, participants move through the four corners creating balance poses with their partners as identified by the four balance formations. Partners work together by pushing or pulling against each other's weight. Remind them to communicate clearly when moving in and out of balances. Encourage partners to hold each pose for three to five seconds. Determine how long participants should work at each corner.

Adaptations

To decrease the challenge:

- Include illustrations or photographs of partner balance poses.
- Increase the time spent at each station.
- Have participants create their own simple balance poses.
- Allow participants to use equipment to help them balance.

To increase the challenge:

- Have participants perform balance poses in groups of three or four.
- Have partners roll a die and balance on that number of body parts.
- Require more challenging balances.
- Add equipment (e.g., beanbags, ribbons, balls) that participants must incorporate into their partner balance poses.

Self-Check Questions
- Am I moving safely in relation to the other participants?
- Do I focus on a spot on the ground or the wall to help me balance?
- Do I manage my body weight along with my partner's over our base of support?
- Am I communicating clearly with my partner?

LINE JUMP

Activity Goal
To perform a variety of jumps over lines on the floor.

Fundamental Movement Skills
Jumping, running, skipping

Tactical Focus
- Demonstrate appropriate movement skills while jumping and landing.
- Develop and apply appropriate strategies to safely jump and land.

Level
Exploring

Facility
Gymnasium

Equipment
Lines (or masking tape) on a gym floor

Time
15 to 20 minutes

Activity Category
Individual pursuits

Safety

Participants should work within their personal limits and perform only jumps that have been taught during instruction. Encourage them to land safely with knees bent. Ensure that indoor activity spaces are free of hazards (e.g., benches, equipment, basketball nets, poles); remove or mark any hazards. Remind participants to keep their heads up and to be aware of others when moving through the space.

Activity Instructions

Prior to the activity, review the criteria for a safe and controlled landing (e.g., feet slightly apart, knees bent, arms extending toward the front, trunk leaning forward slightly with seat tucked under, and core engaged). This activity requires lines on the floor. If lines do not exist, consider creating them with tape.

Participants move through the space in a variety of ways (e.g., running, sliding, skipping) and jump over lines on the floor as they come to them. Participants gradually increase their movement speeds and the height and length of their jumps. Encourage them to jump in a variety of ways (e.g., one-foot and two-foot takeoffs, jumps with turns, jumps that create unique body shapes).

Suggested prompts:

- Can you jump high across a line on the gym floor?
- Can you make small jumps across a line on the gym floor?
- Can you jump over a line with two feet at the same time? With one foot?
- Can you synchronize your jumps with a partner?
- Can you make your body a star shape while jumping?
- Can you jump facing this wall, but land facing that wall?

Adaptations

To decrease the challenge:

- Display photos showing safe takeoffs and landings.
- Photograph or record participants so that they can observe themselves and receive feedback on their jumps and landings.
- Play music and ask participants to jump to the music (fast music for fast jumping, slow music for big, controlled jumps).

To increase the challenge:

- Require more challenging jumps.
- Have participants use different methods of locomotion.
- Add objects to use when traveling (e.g., holding a scarf, balancing a beanbag).

Self-Check Questions

- Am I moving safely during my landings?
- Am I in control of my body during my jumps?
- Do I move safely through the activity area?

BALANCE SHAPES

Activity Goal

To demonstrate a variety of body shapes while performing a static balance pose with a small group.

Fundamental Movement Skill

Balance

Tactical Focus

- Demonstrate appropriate movement skills while perform a static balance pose with a small group.
- Develop and apply appropriate strategies to perform a static balance pose in a small group
- Work collaboratively and communicate effectively with others in a small group.

Level

Exploring

Facility

Gymnasium or outdoors

Equipment

None

Time

15 to 20 minutes

Activity Category

Individual pursuits

Safety

Participants should work within their personal limits and perform only balance poses that have been taught during instruction. Ensure that indoor and outdoor activity spaces are a safe distance from walls and free of hazards (e.g., benches, equipment, basketball nets, holes, loose gravel, wet grass); remove or mark any hazards. Provide safe distances between groups, and remind participants to keep their heads up and to be aware of other groups.

Activity Instructions

Participants form groups of four or five. Call out a shape, object, letter, or number, and have group members work together to use their bodies to create the shape. Consider words, shapes, or objects connected to learning in another area of study or program.

Adaptations

To decrease the challenge:

- Have successful groups share what they are doing to hold their balance.
- Allow group members to hold on to a chair or wall.
- Display photographs of balances.

To increase the challenge:

- Require that groups hold their balances for a longer time.
- Require more challenging balances.
- Pair up participants and have partners take turns telling each other which balance pose to do.

Self-Check Questions

- Am I moving safely in relation to the other participants?
- Am I applying the correct amount of force?
- Am I communicating clearly with my group mates?

Activity Goal

To mirror locomotor movements with a partner.

Fundamental Movement Skills

Running, skipping, jumping, balance

Tactical Focus

- Coordinate body parts while performing movements with a partner.
- Demonstrate a knowledge of how the body is moving in relation to others.
- Work collaboratively and communicate effectively with a partner and in a small group.

Level

Competent

Facility

Gymnasium or outdoors

Equipment

None

Time

15 to 20 minutes

Activity Category

Individual pursuits

Safety

Participants should work within their personal limits and perform only movements that have been taught during instruction. Ensure that indoor and outdoor activity spaces are a safe distance from walls and free of hazards (e.g., benches, equipment, basketball nets, holes, loose gravel, wet grass); remove or mark any hazards. Provide safe distances between partners and groups. Remind participants to keep their heads up and to be aware of others when moving in the space.

Activity Instructions

Working in pairs, participants face each other. One partner is the leader and moves slowly in place while the other mirrors his or her movements. Partners try to synchronize their movements to hide who the leader is. After a given amount of time, participants add traveling movements to their mirroring sequences (e.g., jumping, hopping, sliding, or galloping toward or away from each other). Have leaders switch often.

Next, participants form groups of four and repeat the activity with one participant acting as the leader and the rest following. Have them switch leaders often.

Adaptations

To decrease the challenge:

- Allow participants to select their own simple movements.
- Provide a video of an effective mirroring activity.
- Perform the movements and have the entire group be the mirror. Begin with easy movements.

To increase the challenge:

- Require different methods of locomotion.
- Create larger groups.
- Play music and have the leaders move to the sound or rhythm of the music.

Self-Check Questions

- Am I moving safely in relation to my partner or group?
- Do I use appropriate body parts to move in a specific direction and at a certain level while mirroring my partner or group?
- Do I use effective communication skills while working with my partner or group?
- What did my partner and I say to succeed at this activity?

Activity Goal

To perform a variety of locomotor movements using hula hoops.

Fundamental Movement Skills

Running, jumping, skipping

Tactical Focus

- Develop an awareness of moving safely in relation to others and equipment.
- Develop personal tactics for moving through hula hoops at an optimal challenge level.
- Work collaboratively and communicate effectively with others.

Level

Competent

Facility

Gymnasium or outdoors

Equipment

Hula hoops (1 per participant)

Time

20 to 25 minutes

Activity Category

Individual pursuits

Safety

Participants should work within their personal limits and perform only movements that have been taught during instruction. Ensure that indoor and outdoor activity spaces are a safe distance from walls and free of hazards (e.g., benches, equipment, basketball nets, holes, loose gravel, wet grass); remove or mark any hazards. Provide safe distances between activities occurring in the same space. Remind participants to keep their heads up and to be aware of others when moving through the space.

Activity Instructions

Participants form groups of four or five. Each participant receives one hula hoop. Groups form a straight line and members hold their hoops out to one side at different levels and angles. One at a time, participants drop their hoops and move through, over, under, and around the hoops of the other group members as they make their way from the front of the line to the back before returning to their position in line. Participants use a variety of locomotor patterns as they experiment moving at different levels and in different directions as directed by the hoops.

Next, participants work together to create a locomotor sequence using their own hula hoops to travel together at different levels and in different pathways and directions simultaneously.

Adaptations

To decrease the challenge:

- Use larger hula hoops.
- Use half the number of hoops as participants.
- Use pool noodles instead of hoops.

To increase the challenge:

- Use smaller hula hoops.
- Increase the speed at which participants must move through the line.
- Do not allow participants to repeat a mode of traveling.
- Have groups challenge each other to see which group moves through the hula hoops the fastest.

Self-Check Questions

- Am I moving safely in relation to equipment and the other participants?
- Do I communicate effectively with others in my group?
- Do I use personal tactics for moving through the hula hoops?

MOVEMENT STATIONS ON AND OFF EQUIPMENT

Activity Goal

To perform a variety of station activities exploring locomotor movements on and off equipment.

Fundamental Movement Skill

Balance, coordination

Tactical Focus

- Move safely using a variety of movements.
- Coordinate parts of the body while performing the station activities.
- Understand one's own strengths and areas in need of improvement when participating in station activities.

Level

Competent

Facility

Gymnasium

Equipment

4 benches, 15 to 20 mats, 10 station cards

Time

35 to 40 minutes

Activity Category

Individual pursuits

Safety

Participants should work within their personal limits and perform only balance poses and rolls that have been taught during instruction. Ensure that indoor activity spaces are free of hazards (e.g., benches, equipment, basketball nets, poles); remove or mark any hazards. Provide safe distances between stations, and remind participants to keep their heads up and to be aware of others.

Activity Instructions

Prior to the activity, set up the following stations. At each station, provide a description, safety considerations, and an illustration or photograph.

Participants form groups of four or five that are positioned at different stations. Review station activities and safety considerations before they begin. Determine how much time groups should remain at each station.

- Station 1: Shoulder roll
- Station 2: Back roll
- Station 3: Front support balance
- Station 4: Cartwheel
- Station 5: Bridge
- Station 6: Tripod balance
- Station 7: V-sit on a bench
- Station 8: Front scale balance on a bench
- Station 9: Turn on a bench
- Station 10: Jump using a variety of body shapes off a bench

Adaptations

To decrease the challenge:

- Allow participants to select the stations to complete.
- Have participants work in pairs to help each other balance.
- Increase the time spent at each station.

To increase the challenge:

- Have participants select challenging variations of station moves.
- Have each participant select a favorite station and create a movement sequence that includes the station activity.
- Add equipment at each station (e.g. balance ball, balance pods, ribbons).

Self-Check Questions

- Am I moving safely using a variety of movements?
- Am I able to coordinate parts of my body while performing the station activities?
- Do I understand my own strengths and areas in need of improvement when participating in station activities?

Activity Goal

To hold static balance poses.

Fundamental Movement Skill

Balance

Tactical Focus

- Demonstrate appropriate movement skills while holding static balance poses (e.g., extending arms to the side to increase stability while balancing, being aware of one's body in relation to others).
- Develop and apply appropriate strategies to maintain balance (e.g., engage the core, keep the eyes on a stationary point).

Level

Competent

Facility

Gymnasium

Equipment

None

Time

10 to 15 minutes

Activity Category

Individual pursuits

Safety

Participants should work within their personal limits and perform only balance poses that have been taught during instruction. Ensure that indoor activity spaces are free of hazards (e.g., benches, equipment, basketball nets, poles); remove or mark any hazards. Remind participants to keep their heads up and to be aware of others when moving through the space.

Activity Instructions

Participants move through the activity space in a variety of ways (e.g., running, skipping, jumping) and slowly decrease intensity and speed until they freeze in a balance pose. They then perform a series of balances in slow motion. Encourage them to hold their positions for 10 to 15 seconds, without moving, before moving into the next balance pose. Encourage participants to balance on different body parts and at different levels.

Adaptations

To decrease the challenge:

- Permit participants to hold on to a chair or wall to help them balance.
- Display photographs of balance positions.

To increase the challenge:

- Have participants use different methods of locomotion.
- Require more challenging balance poses.
- Have participants travel through the area in pairs.

Self-Check Questions

- Am I moving safely through the activity space?
- Do I extend my arms to the side to increase stability during my balance?
- Do I keep my eyes on a stationary point while balancing?

LEAN ON ME

Activity Goal

To hold a static balance pose with a small group.

Fundamental Movement Skills

Balance, running, skipping, jumping

Tactical Focus

- Demonstrate appropriate movement skills while holding a static balance pose with a small group (e.g., extending arms to the side to increase stability while balancing, being aware of one's body in relation to group mates).

- Develop and apply appropriate strategies to maintain balance with a small group (e.g., engage the core, keep the eyes on a stationary point, communicate with the group).

Level
Proficient

Facility
Gymnasium

Equipment
2 dice

Time
15 to 20 minutes

Activity Category
Individual pursuits

Safety
Participants should work within their personal limits and perform only balance poses that have been taught during instruction. Ensure that indoor activity spaces are free of hazards (e.g., benches, equipment, basketball nets, poles); remove or mark any hazards. Provide safe distances between groups, and remind participants to keep their heads up and to be aware of others when moving through the space.

Activity Instructions
Participants move through the activity space in a variety of ways (e.g., running, skipping, jumping). Roll a die to determine the number of participants in each group that must hold a balance pose. State whether the pose should be back to back, shoulder to shoulder, or front to front, and whether it should be a pushing or pulling pose. Groups, in the size directed by the die roll, hold the position for three or four seconds. Participants should try to work with different groups each round.

Adaptations

To decrease the challenge:

- Have one or two successful groups share the strategies they are using to maintain their balance.
- Allow group members to hold on to a chair or wall.
- Display photographs of balances.
- Roll two dice. The first determines the number of participants in a group; the second determines the number of body parts that should touch the ground.

To increase the challenge:

- Roll a second die to determine the number of body parts the group should balance on.
- Require that participants close one or both eyes while holding their balance.
- Have participants use different methods of locomotion.
- Require more challenging balance poses.

Self-Check Questions

- Am I moving safely in relation to the other participants?
- Am I applying the correct amount of force?
- Am I communicating clearly with my group mates?

YOU OR ME

Activity Goal

Participants hold a balance while their partner provides movements over, under, or through their held pose.

Fundamental Movement Skill

Balance

Tactical Focus

- Demonstrate appropriate movement skills while holding a static balance pose (e.g., extending arms to the side to increase stability while balancing, being aware of one's body in relation to others).
- Develop and apply appropriate strategies to maintain balance (e.g., engage the core, keep the eyes on a stationary point, communicate with a partner).

- Demonstrate a variety of locomotor movements while working with a partner.

Level
Proficient

Facility
Gymnasium

Equipment
None

Time
15 to 20 minutes

Activity Category
Individual pursuits

Safety
Participants should work within their personal limits and perform only balance poses that have been taught during instruction. Ensure that indoor activity spaces are free of hazards (e.g., benches, equipment, basketball nets, poles); remove or mark any hazards. Provide safe distances between partners, and remind them to keep their heads up and to be aware of others when moving through the space.

Activity Instructions
Participants, in pairs and standing face to face, decide who will follow the directions of "me" and who will follow the directions of "you." Participants begin by performing physical tasks in place (e.g., jumping jack, squat). Call out either "Me" or "You" followed by one of the following tasks:
- Go over: Participants move safely over their partners, who hold a low static balance pose.
- Go through: Participants safely move through their partners' open legs as they hold a wide static balance pose.
- Go around: Participants quickly run around their partners, who hold a narrow static balance pose.

Participants complete the task; then quickly return to performing the in-place physical task. After a few rounds, consider calling out multiple tasks in a row: "Me: go over; me: go under; you: go over."

Adaptations

To decrease the challenge:

- Allow participants to choose their own physical tasks.
- Permit group members to hold on to a chair or wall for balance.
- Display photographs of balances.

To increase the challenge:

- Have participants close one or both eyes while balancing.
- Have participants use different methods of locomotion.
- Require more challenging balance poses.

Self-Check Questions

- Am I moving safely in relation to my partner?
- Am I moving quickly around my partner?
- Do I demonstrate appropriate movement skills while holding a static balance pose?
- Do I apply appropriate strategies to hold my balance?

ROTATION STATIONS

Activity Goal

To perform station activities exploring a variety of rotations including rolls and turns.

Fundamental Movement Skill

Coordination

Tactical Focus

- Move safely using a variety of locomotor movements.
- Coordinate parts of the body while performing the station activities.
- Understand one's own strengths and areas in need of improvement when participating in station activities.

Level

Proficient

Facility

Gymnasium

Equipment

10 to 15 mats, poster paper, markers

Time

40 to 45 minutes

Activity Category

Individual pursuits

Safety

Participants should work within their personal limits and perform only rolls that have been taught during instruction. Ensure that indoor activity spaces are free of hazards (e.g., benches, equipment, basketball nets, poles); remove or mark any hazards. Provide safe distances between stations, and remind participants to keep their heads up and to be aware of others when working at and moving between stations.

Activity Instructions

Prior to the activity, set up the following stations. Include a description of the station, safety considerations, and possibly an illustration or photograph.

Participants form groups of four or five. Each group begins at a different station. Review station activities and safety considerations before they begin.

- Station 1: Egg roll. Lower yourself sideways over your knees onto your shoulder; then onto your back and over to your other shoulder to return to a low squat, tucked in a tight ball position on your feet.

- Station 2: Log roll. Lie on the mat with your arms stretched out over your head. Keep your body straight and tightly activated through your core. Use your entire body to turn as you roll down the mat.

- Station 3: Forward roll. Squat and tuck, facing the mat in a tight ball position with your knees hugged in toward your chest and your feet together. Place your fingers on the mat pointed toward the end of the mat with your elbows pointing out. Tuck your chin toward your chest. Lift your hips while straightening your legs, and bend your arms to roll onto the back of your shoulders. Continue in a tucked formation throughout the roll; then reach forward with your arms as you stand up, with your feet together and body tight.

- Station 4: Shoulder roll. Squat and tuck, facing the mat in a tight ball position with your knees hugged in toward your chest and your feet together. Place your fingers on the mat pointed toward the end of the mat with your elbows pointing out. Tuck your chin toward your chest. Roll onto your shoulder, not the back of your head. Tuck your arms under your body when rolling. Continue in a tucked formation throughout the roll; then reach forward with your arms as you stand up, with your feet together and body tight.

- Station 5: Back roll. Stand with your back toward the mat. Squat and tuck into a tight ball position with your knees hugged in toward your chest and your feet together. Place your hands with palms toward the ceiling. Roll onto your back with your legs up and over your head. Push with your arms to get your head off the floor to reduce the pressure on your neck and help rotate your body to return to standing. Use momentum to help with rolling over your neck.

- Station 6: Half turn. Stand tall and jump up, reaching both arms above your head to help with momentum. Land safely on the same spot you jumped from, bending your knees.

- Station 7: Straddle roll. Stand tall with your legs wide apart. Place your hands on the mat between your legs. Roll forward keeping your legs in a straddle position. Following the rotation, place your hands on the mat between your legs to push your body up and over into a standing position or a second roll.

- Station 8: Pike roll. Stand tall with your legs tightly together. Fold at your waist with your chin tucked in. Place the back of your head on the mat and roll, keeping your legs straight and folded forward at the waist. As you roll forward, stay in the folded pike position with straight legs. After the rotation, push hard with your hands on the mat to push yourself to standing while keeping your legs straight.

- Station 9: Donkey kick. Place your hands on the mat. Take your weight onto your hands by kicking both of your legs back and up, trying to keep them as straight as possible.

  Safety: Your back should not arch.

- Station 10: Cartwheel. Standing tall, keep your head between your arms. Keep your arms straight as you reach toward the floor demonstrating the cue pattern *Hand, hand, foot, foot.* Point your toes and keep your legs straight.

Adaptations

To decrease the challenge:

- Permit participants to select which stations to complete.
- Have participants work in pairs.
- Increase the time spent at each station.

To increase the challenge:

- Require that participants select challenging variations of station activities.
- Have participants combine two or more rotations in a sequence.
- Have participants select a favorite station and create a movement sequence that includes the station activity.

Self-Check Questions

- Am I moving safely using a variety of movements?
- Am I able to coordinate parts of my body while performing the station activities?
- Do I understand my own strengths and areas in need of improvement when participating in station activities?

CHAPTER 4

Creative Movement

This chapter provides opportunities to develop and sequence independent movement skills with the fundamental movement skills of running, jumping, balance, agility, and coordination, while also learning movement concepts. Participants demonstrate a variety of creative locomotor movements as they travel alone, with partners, or in small groups while exploring the movement concepts of body, space, effort, and relationships. They also move creatively in response to counting, literature, personal expression, themes, music, and equipment. Communicating with partners and group members and traveling safely through the activity space are also emphasized.

Words to Know

- **Agility.** The ability to change direction in an efficient and effective manner using a combination of balance (static and dynamic), speed, strength, and coordination.
- **Body awareness.** An awareness of the body parts that are moving, and how they are moving (e.g., shapes, actions).
- **Coordination.** The ability to use multiple parts of the body together in a controlled manner.
- **Dynamic balance.** The ability to use core strength to maintain balance and body control while moving through space (e.g., turning, rolling, balancing, landing from a jump).
- **Effort awareness.** An awareness of how the body moves (e.g., time, force, flow).
- **Frontal plane.** A vertical plane that divides the body into front and back.
- **Horizontal plane.** A traverse plane that divides the body into top and bottom.
- **Jumping and landing.** The act of moving off a surface and into the air using two feet. A jump includes three phases: takeoff (preparation), flight (execution), and landing (follow-through).
- **Relationship.** An awareness of the people, objects, or environmental features (e.g., music) one is moving with.
- **Running.** Moving quickly using the legs in such a way that both feet are simultaneously off the ground for an instant.
- **Sagittal plane.** The vertical plane that divides the body into left and right.
- **Spatial awareness.** An awareness of one's own body in space (e.g., location, direction, level, pathway, plane, extensions).
- **Static balance.** The ability to maintain a desired shape while in a stationary position (e.g., V-sit, stork stand, T-scale).

Balance Transferable Skills

Balance

1. Focus on a stationary object (e.g., a point on the wall or floor).
2. Keep a tight body (e.g., maintain body control).
3. Keep body weight low and centered over the base of support.

Jumping and Landing Transferable Skills

Preparation	Execution	Follow-Through
1. Bend the knees. 2. Swing the arms forward with appropriate force to help move the body forward and up.	Keep the body tight.	1. Bend the knees to absorb the landing. 2. Keep the feet shoulder-width apart. 3. Hold the arms out for balance. 4. Keep the head up.

Jumping and landing learning cues: Bend the knees, swing the arms back and forward, extend the legs and feet at takeoff, land softly.

Rotation Transferable Skills

Jump Turn

1. Bend the knees.
2. Stand tall, jump up, reach both arms above the head, rotate halfway or all the way around.
3. Land safely, bending the knees.

Jump turn learning cues: Bend the knees, jump for height, stretch the arms above the head, maintain balance, land softly.

Forward Roll

1. Squat and tuck facing the mat in a tight ball position with knees hugged in toward the chest and feet together.
2. Place fingers on the mat pointed toward the end of the mat with elbows pointing out.
3. Tuck the chin toward the chest.
4. Lift the hips while straightening the legs and bending the arms to roll on the back of the shoulders.
5. Continue in a tucked formation throughout the roll; then reach forward while standing up, with feet together and body tight.

Forward roll learning cues: Tuck facing the mat, hug the knees in a tight ball, tuck the chin toward the chest, lift the hips, roll on the back of the shoulders, stay tucked throughout the roll, stand up with a tight body.

Running Transferable Skills

Upper-Body Position	Lower-Body Position
1. Center the head between the shoulders and look ahead.	1. Lift the knees high.
2. Relax the jaw and neck.	2. Contact the ground with a midfoot or heel strike under the body's center of gravity.
3. Lean slightly forward.	3. Push off the ground with the ball of the foot.
4. Keep the shoulders relaxed and parallel to the ground.	
5. Lightly cup the hands.	
6. Bend the elbows at approximately 90 degrees.	
7. Swing the arms backward and forward from the shoulders. Don't let them cross the midline of the body.	
8. Move the arms and legs in opposition.	

Running learning cues: Keep the hands relaxed, bend the elbows, swing forward and back, keep a tall body, run softly.

Where's the Physical Literacy?

Creative movement allows participants to develop physical literacy by exploring fundamental movement skills and movement concepts in expressive ways. As they learn, refine, extend, and apply movement concepts (e.g., body, space, effort, and relationships) and sequence fundamental movement skills, they express ideas and emotions through movement.

Through an exploration of body awareness, participants address the movement of body parts alone and in combination, as well as the shapes and actions body parts can take and perform. They also become aware of the locations, directions, levels, and pathways of their movements. In more advanced activities, participants explore planes of movement as well as extensions into space. Through effort awareness, participants become more aware of how the body moves in terms of time, force, and flow. Finally, participants learn about relationships as they travel through space while considering people, objects, and environmental elements such as counting, props, and music.

Through creative movement, participants expand their movement experiences with imagination and creativity as they learn to travel through space confidently and competently.

Educator Check and Reflect

- Display choreography, locomotor movements, or movement concepts for reference.
- Use participant movement sequences for warm-ups and cool-downs throughout the year.
- Use music with a strong beat and have participants practice finding the beat (e.g., by clapping, stomping, moving through space, speaking on the beat), when appropriate.
- Review all music for appropriate language and message.
- Use a variety of music genres (including novel and popular music).
- Integrate local community and cultural traditions into movement sequences through choreography, music, props, or special guests.
- Encourage participants to work with different partners and group members.
- As appropriate, teach choreographed movement sequences in manageable segments.

Activity Goal

To move throughout the activity space using a variety of speeds, levels, pathways, and directions.

Fundamental Movement Skills

Agility, coordination

Tactical Focus

- Travel through space using a variety of speeds (e.g., slow, medium, fast).
- Travel through space at different levels (e.g., low, medium, high).
- Travel through space using a variety of pathways (e.g., zigzag, straight, curved, wavy).
- Travel through space using a variety of directions (e.g., forward, backward, sideways, diagonally, up, down, left, right).

Level

Beginning

Facility

Gymnasium or outdoors

Equipment

None

Time

10 to 15 minutes

Activity Category

Individual pursuits

Safety

Ensure that the activity space is a safe distance from hazards (e.g., walls, equipment, debris); remove or mark any hazards. Remind participants to keep their heads up and to be aware of others when moving through the space.

Activity Instructions

Participants scatter throughout the activity space. Encourage them to move throughout the space using a variety of speeds, levels, pathways, and directions. Ask them: Can you . . .

- Run quickly but softly in a straight line? In a curved line?
- Hop sideways? To the left? To the right? Low to the ground?
- Crawl close to the ground like a snake? Move forward? Move backward?
- Gallop in a straight line while changing directions whenever you meet a classmate?
- Fly like an airplane moving quickly in curved paths?
- Walk tall like a long-legged clown on stilts? Walk backward?
- Make your body wiggle like jelly? Wiggle only your hand? Arm? Belly? Leg?
- Do a straight movement with your arms? Your knees? Your head?
- Leap high over a rock? Long over a puddle? Quickly over a snake?
- Gallop like a pony in a zigzag formation?
- Walk slowly as if you have just landed on the moon? Walk on the moon sideways? Backward? In a curved formation?

Adaptations

To decrease the challenge:

- Have participants travel while moving fewer body parts.
- Require only forward and backward movements.
- Have participants reduce their speed while performing each activity.

To increase the challenge:

- Require that participants move many body parts at once.
- Have participants move at different heights.
- Place participants in pairs or small groups.
- Have participants use an implement (e.g., bounce a ball, balance a beanbag) while performing locomotion movements.

Self-Check Questions

- Can I move using a variety of speeds (e.g., slow, medium, fast)?
- Am I able to perform movements at different levels (e.g., low, medium, high)?

- Can I travel using a variety of pathways (e.g., zigzag, straight, curved, wavy)?
- Can I travel in a variety of directions (e.g., forward, backward, sideways, diagonally, up, down, left, right)?

WHICH PART LEADS?

Activity Goal

To travel through space using a variety of locomotor movement led by specific body parts.

Fundamental Movement Skills

Agility, coordination, running, jumping

Tactical Focus

- Perform locomotor movements using specific body parts (e.g., arms, legs, elbows, knees, head).
- Travel safely in relation to other participants.

Level

Beginning

Facility

Gymnasium or outdoors

Equipment

8 to 10 body part cards, 8 to 10 locomotor movement cards

Time

10 to 15 minutes

Activity Category

Individual pursuits

Safety

Ensure that the activity space is a safe distance from hazards (e.g., walls, equipment, debris); remove or mark any hazards. Remind participants to keep their heads up and to be aware of others when moving through the space.

Activity Instructions

Prior to beginning the activity, create two sets of cards: one that lists body parts (e.g., finger, nose, knees, head, abdomen, back, toe) and one (preferably a different color) that lists locomotor movements (e.g., run, skip, hop, slide, walk, gallop).

As participants move throughout the activity space, select one card from each deck and call out the locomotor movement and the body part that will lead the movement. Participants then move throughout the activity space using the movement and leading with the body part until you choose a second pair of cards. Once cards are pulled, place them back in the piles. Consider letting participants select the cards. Draw attention to those who are moving in creative and unique ways.

Adaptations

To decrease the challenge:

- Decrease the activity level of the locomotor movement activities.
- Call out simple, or smaller, body parts.
- Have participants travel with slow and sustained effort.
- Call the locomotor movement first, and then add the body part.

To increase the challenge:

- Increase the number of body parts used.
- Have participants move using a variety of body shapes (e.g., wide, narrow, round, stretched, twisted, symmetrical, asymmetrical).

- Have participants work with partners. One partner moves throughout the space with a body part leading. The other imitates the movement while trying to guess which body part is leading. Partners switch roles after each correct guess.
- Create an additional set of cards that show objects (e.g., beanbag, ball, skipping rope, scarf) that are available to the group. Pull a card from each of the three decks; participants must perform the movement with the body part leading and also include the object in a creative way.

Self-Check Questions

- Am I moving safely in relation to the other participants?
- Can I perform locomotor movements using specific body parts (e.g., arms, legs, elbows, knees, head)?
- Do I understand what body parts to move and how?

ADD UP MOVES

Activity Goal

To perform a variety of locomotor movements based on the roll of a die.

Fundamental Movement Skills

Agility, balance, coordination, running, jumping

Tactical Focus

- Travel in response to external stimuli.
- Travel in different directions (e.g., forward, backward, sideways).
- Travel in different body shapes (e.g., wide, narrow, stretched, curled, twisted).

Level

Beginning

Facility

Gymnasium or outdoors

Equipment

Poster paper, markers, five to eight dice (one per group)

Time

10 to 15 minutes

Activity Category

Individual pursuits

Safety

Ensure that the activity space is a safe distance from hazards (e.g., walls, equipment, debris); remove or mark any hazards. Provide safe distances between groups working in the same space. Remind participants to keep their heads up and be aware of others when moving through the space.

Activity Instructions

Prior to the activity, brainstorm with participants a variety of locomotor movements (e.g., walk, skip, hop, run, jump, gallop, leap, slide). Consider recording these responses on poster paper for reference.

Divide participants into groups of four or five, and give each group one die. Groups select five or six movements from the poster paper; then roll the die to determine how many repetitions of each movement they will perform (e.g., after rolling a 4, participants walk 4 steps forward). Groups add directions and body shapes to their selected movements. Group members then practice the moves in a sequence (e.g., walk forward for 4 steps stretched tall, skip backward for 6 steps low to the ground, slide sideways for 1 step, gallop diagonally for 4 steps, and run in a circle for 6 steps with a wide body shape).

Adaptations

To decrease the challenge:

- Provide a routine for participants to follow.
- Have groups include only two or three movements in their sequences.
- Have participants record their sequences for reference while performing.
- Have the entire group create a routine so all participants understand the expectations.

To increase the challenge:

- Increase the intensity of the locomotor movements.
- Require that participants move using different levels of force (e.g., light, strong).

- Have group members travel together throughout their sequence (e.g., follow, lead, mirror, shadow, move in unison).
- Add equipment (e.g., scarves, wooden dowels, ribbons).

Self-Check Questions
- Am I able to move simultaneously with my group?
- Am I able to move in different directions (e.g., forward, backward, sideways)?
- Can I move in different shapes (e.g., wide, narrow, stretched, curled, twisted)?

STORYBOOK MOVEMENTS

Activity Goal
To move using a variety of speeds, levels, pathways, and directions while recreating characters from familiar stories.

Fundamental Movement Skills
Agility, balance, coordination, running, jumping

Tactical Focus
- Travel using a variety of speeds (e.g., slow, medium, fast).
- Perform movements at different levels (e.g., low, medium, high).
- Travel using a variety of pathways (e.g., zigzag, straight, curved, wavy).
- Travel in a variety of directions (e.g., forward, backward, sideways, diagonally, up, down, left, right).

Level
Exploring

Facility
Gymnasium or outdoors

Equipment
The group's favorite storybooks, poetry, movies, video games

Time

10 to 15 minutes

Activity Category

Individual pursuits

Safety

Ensure that the activity space is a safe distance from hazards (e.g., walls, equipment, debris); remove or mark any hazards. Remind participants to keep their heads up and be aware of others when moving through the space.

Activity Instructions

Prior to the activity, review with participants characters from classroom books, stories, or movies, or characters from their favorite storybook, poem, movie, or video game. Consider recording their characters on poster paper, or bringing the storybooks or character photographs to the activity area.

As prompted, participants move throughout the activity space imitating their favorite characters. Ask them: Can you move like . . .

- A basketball player about to take the winning shot?
- A wicked witch riding on a broomstick?
- A deer in the woods that senses danger?
- A sport team that won the championship?
- A sport team that lost the championship?
- A traveler lost in a new city?
- A scuba diver, underwater, discovering lost treasure?
- A small seed slowly growing into a flower?
- A hungry shark looking for dinner?
- A rabbit being chased by a fox?
- A fox chasing a rabbit?
- A palm tree blowing in a wind storm?

Adaptations

To decrease the challenge:

- Display locomotor movements along with movement concepts (e.g., pathways, speeds, levels, timing) on poster paper for reference.
- Have participants choose words from the poster paper and match them with their characters while performing the activity.

- Have participants travel in pairs, taking turns leading and following.
- Reduce the intensity of the locomotor movements.

To increase the challenge:

- Have participants perform locomotor movements in relation to objects (e.g., over, under, beside, on).
- Have participants memorize familiar poems, songs, or short stories, and have half the group recite the work while the other half moves to the words.
- Place participants in pairs. One partner chooses a character and moves throughout the space as that character; the other imitates the actions while trying to guess the character. Partners switch roles after each correct guess.
- Add equipment (e.g., scarves, wooden dowels, ribbons).

Self-Check Questions

- Do I move using a variety of speeds (e.g., slow, medium, fast)?
- Am I able to perform movements at different levels (e.g., low, medium, high)?
- Can I travel using a variety of pathways (e.g., zigzag, straight, curved, wavy)?
- Do I travel in a variety of directions (e.g., forward, backward, sideways, diagonally, up, down, left, right)?

FOUR-WAY DANCE-OFF

Activity Goal

To work in a small group performing locomotor movements in response to various genres of music.

Fundamental Movement Skills

Agility, balance, coordination

Tactical Focus

- Perform movements using a variety of body parts.
- Perform smooth transfers of movement.
- Change movements in response to external stimuli.
- Perform movements using a variety of levels, times, speeds, and pathways.

Level

Exploring

Facility

Gymnasium or outdoors

Equipment

Music and audio equipment

Time

15 to 20 minutes

Activity Category

Individual pursuits

Safety

Ensure that the activity space is a safe distance from walls and free of hazards (e.g., benches, equipment, basketball nets, holes, loose gravel, wet grass); remove or mark any hazards. Provide safe distances between groups. Remind participants to keep their heads up and to be aware of others.

Activity Instructions

Participants form groups of four and stand in a diamond formation. Play a variety of genres of music (e.g., reggae, country, pop, rap, classical, dubstep). Participants face the front of the activity space and imitate the group member at the front of the diagonal, who is moving in response to the music. After a designated amount of time, change the music and have groups face another wall and follow the new leader.

Adaptations

To decrease the challenge:

- Prior to the activity, brainstorm movements to perform in response to various genres of music.
- Prior to the activity, review how movements can be modified when the genre of the music changes. Have participants practice modifying their movements.
- Display movements on poster paper for reference.
- Reduce the time participants spend as the leader.

To increase the challenge:

- Increase the intensity of the movements.
- Have groups perform various group movements (e.g., follow, lead, mirror, shadow, move in unison).
- Add equipment (e.g., scarves, wooden dowels, ribbons).

Self-Check Questions

- Am I moving a variety of body parts?
- Can I perform smooth transfers of movement?
- Am I able to change my movements in response to different music?
- Am I incorporating levels, time, speed, and pathways in my movements?

EXPLORING DIRECTION DANCE STATIONS

Activity Goal

To move through locomotor movement stations that focus on traveling in different directions.

Fundamental Movement Skills

Agility, balance, coordination

Tactical Focus

- Travel safely in relation to the other participants.
- Travel using a variety of body parts at each station.
- Perform movements in a variety of directions (e.g., forward, backward, sideways, diagonally, up, down, left, right).

Level

Exploring

Facility

Gymnasium or outdoors

Equipment

Music and audio equipment

Time
15 to 20 minutes

Activity Category
Individual pursuits

Safety
Ensure that the activity space is a safe distance from walls and free of hazards (e.g., benches, equipment, basketball nets, holes, loose gravel, wet grass); remove or mark any hazards. Provide safe distances between stations. Remind participants to keep their heads up and to be aware of others when moving through the space.

Activity Instructions
Prior to the activity, create 8 to 10 movement stations throughout the activity space. At each station post both text and an illustration of the station task.

Ensure that participants have sufficient space to move around safely. Review station activities and safety with participants prior to beginning. Participants select their first stations, ensuring relatively the same numbers at all stations. Participants spend two or three minutes at each station. When the music stops, everyone moves clockwise to the next station.

Consider the following station ideas:
- Explore ways to move forward.
- Explore ways to move forward at a low level.
- Explore ways to move backward.
- Explore ways to move backward at a low level.
- Explore ways to move sideways.
- Explore ways to move sideways at a high level.
- Explore ways to move diagonally.
- Explore ways to move diagonally very slowly.
- Explore ways to move up and down.
- Explore ways to move in a curved way.

Adaptations
To decrease the challenge:
- Decrease the intensity of the assigned stations.
- Allow more time at each station.
- Allow participants to select which stations they complete.

To increase the challenge:

- Have participants explore moving different body parts (e.g., head, shoulders, arms, hands, legs, feet).
- Require that participants move at different levels (e.g., low, medium, high).
- Have participants combine movements at each station.
- Place participants in pairs or small groups and have them complete the station tasks together.
- Add equipment (e.g., scarves, wooden dowels, ribbons).

Self-Check Questions

- Am I moving safely in relation to the other participants?
- Am I using a variety of body parts at each station?
- Do I perform my movements in a variety of directions (e.g., forward, backward, sideways, diagonally, up, down, left, right)?

MOVING A ROUND

Activity Goal

To perform a variety of locomotor movements using a hula hoop.

Fundamental Movement Skills

Agility, coordination, jumping

Tactical Focus

- Transition smoothly from one move to the next.
- Maintain control of the hula hoop.
- Work collaboratively with group members.

Level

Exploring

Facility

Gymnasium or outdoors

Equipment

20 to 30 hula hoops (one per participant), 5 to 7 dice (one per group)

Time
15 to 20 minutes

Activity Category
Individual pursuits

Safety
Ensure that the activity space is a safe distance from walls and free of hazards (e.g., benches, equipment, basketball nets, holes, loose gravel, wet grass); remove or mark any hazards. Provide safe distances between groups. Remind participants to keep their heads up and to be aware of others.

Activity Instructions
Prior to the activity, use poster paper to create a poster with numbers (1 through 6) and corresponding hula hoop movements. Consider creating the poster with participants.

Participants form groups of four or five, which scatter throughout the activity area. Each participant receives one hula hoop, and each group receives one die. Group members take turns rolling the die to choose the hula hoop movements that everyone performs.

Following are possible movements:

- Travel low as you move around the hula hoop.
- Swing the hula hoop around different parts of the body.
- Travel high as you move over the hula hoop.
- Travel through the hula hoop with different parts of the body leading.
- Travel over the hula hoop at different speeds.
- Toss and catch the hula hoop while moving at different heights.

Adaptations
To decrease the challenge:

- Use hula hoops of different sizes.
- Allow participants to create their own movements to correspond to each die number.
- Include illustrations (or student photographs) of movements on the poster.

To increase the challenge:

- Increase the complexity of the movements.
- Have groups select their favorite moves and create a routine that combines them.

- Have groups perform various group movements (e.g., follow, lead, mirror, shadow, echo, move in unison).
- Place participants in pairs and have them perform the movements with one hula hoop.

Self-Check Questions

- Am I transitioning smoothly from one move to the next?
- Do I maintain control of the hula hoop?
- Do I communicate well with other group members?
- Am I able to perform a variety of locomotor movements with objects (e.g., moving over, under, beside, through)?

PARTNER MOVES

Activity Goal

To perform a variety of locomotor movements both independently and with a partner while responding to music or a theme.

Fundamental Movement Skills

Agility, coordination

Tactical Focus

- Move safely in relation to others.
- Perform smooth transitions between movements.
- Perform a variety of locomotor movements in relation to a partner (e.g., meet, part, match, contrast, follow, lead, unison, echo).

Level

Competent

Facility

Gymnasium or outdoors

Equipment

Music and audio equipment

Time

15 to 20 minutes

Activity Category

Individual pursuits

Safety

Ensure that the activity space is a safe distance from walls and free of hazards (e.g., benches, equipment, basketball nets, holes, loose gravel, wet grass); remove or mark any hazards. Remind participants to keep their heads up and to be aware of others when moving through the space.

Activity Instructions

Prior to the activity, review partner dance movements with participants. Consider recording movements on poster paper for participant reference.

Participants scatter throughout the activity area and dance in response to either m usic (e.g., country, folk) or a life theme (e.g., happiness, family, community). On your signal, everyone finds a partner.

In pairs, participants perform a partner dance movement that you indicate verbally or by referencing optional poster paper. On your signal, participants leave their partners and continue to move independently throughout the space.

Following are suggested partner dance moves:

- Two-hand turn: Participants hold hands and walk in a circle.
- Around the world: Participants hold hands and turn in a circle lifting their arms above their heads and not letting go.
- Elbow swing: Participants link elbows and skip in a circle.
- Two-hand swing: Participants hold hands and, while leaning back, skip in a circle. Remind participants to move safely and not to run.
- Do-si-do: Participants face each other and walk forward passing right shoulders, step sideways to the right passing back to back, and walk backward to return to their original positions. Have participants practice on both sides.
- Clapping sequence: For a total of 8 counts, participants slap their thighs twice, clap their hands twice, clap right hands with a partner twice, and clap left hands with a partner twice.
- Forward and backward sway: Partners stand face-to-face; one partner leans forward while the other leans backward, and then they switch.
- Forward and backward strut: Participants walk four steps away from their partners and four steps toward their partners.
- Promenade: Partners walk side by side holding right hands (the participant on the right side crosses their right arm in front). The partner on the left places their left hand on their own left shoulder, which the other partner holds with their left hand by reaching

across their partner's back. When changing directions, both partners turn to the left.

Adaptations

To decrease the challenge:

- Display photographs of partner dance movements for reference.
- Use equipment such as scarves or wooden dowels to connect partners.
- Have participants perform the dance movements alone first before progressing to working with a partner.

To increase the challenge:

- Increase the intensity of the movements.
- Have partners create sequences using the moves they explored during the activity.
- Invite participants to explore how the partner dance movements would look with more than two participants.
- Add equipment (e.g., scarves, wooden dowels, ribbons).

Self-Check Questions

- Am I moving safely in relation to my partner?
- Am I performing smooth transitions between movements?
- Do I perform a variety of locomotor movements in relation to my partner (e.g., meet, part, match, contrast, follow, lead, unison, echo)?

MOVING TRIANGLE

Activity Goal

To explore the concept of space while traveling in relation to a small group.

Fundamental Movement Skills

Agility, balance, coordination, running, jumping

Tactical Focus

- Travel safely in relation to others.
- Hold a balance using a variety of body parts.
- Perform movements using a variety of spatial concepts (e.g., changes in location, level, direction, pathway, and plane).

Level

Competent

Facility

Gymnasium or outdoors

Equipment

None

Time

15 to 20 minutes

Activity Category

Individual pursuits

Safety

Ensure that the activity space is a safe distance from walls and free of hazards (e.g., benches, equipment, basketball nets, holes, loose gravel, wet grass); remove or mark any hazards. Remind participants to keep their heads up and to be aware of others when moving through the space.

Activity Instructions

Participants scatter throughout the activity space, and each one secretly selects two partners. Participants do not share who their partners are. On your signal, everyone moves throughout the activity space frequently changing locations, levels, directions, pathways, and planes. While traveling, they attempt to maintain equal distances between their partners. When participants find themselves forming an equilateral triangle with their two secret partners, they stop moving and hold a balance pose. If either secret partner begins to move again, the participant must move to adjust the triangle. The activity concludes when all participants have stopped moving and are holding a balance pose.

Adaptations

To decrease the challenge:

- Decrease the intensity of the movements.
- Focus on only a couple of spatial concepts (e.g., changes in location and level).
- Reduce the time spent on task.

To increase the challenge:

- Have participants balance on a variety of body parts.
- Increase the speed of movements.
- Have participants change locomotor movements often.

Self-Check Questions

- Am I moving safely in relation to the other participants?
- Am I able to hold a balance using a variety of body parts?
- Do I perform my movements using a variety of spatial concepts (e.g., changes in location, level, direction, pathway, and plane)?

COMIC BOOK MOVES

Activity Goal

To perform a variety of locomotor movements in response to comic book action words while traveling through space.

Fundamental Movement Skills

Agility, balance, coordination, running, jumping

Tactical Focus

- Move safely in relation to others.
- Perform movements using a variety of spatial concepts (e.g., changes in location, level, direction, pathway, and plane).
- Demonstrate a variety of amounts of force using body movement (e.g., light and strong).

Level

Competent

Facility

Gymnasium or outdoors

Equipment

Magazines (including comic books or graphic novels), poster paper, marker

Time
15 to 20 minutes

Activity Category
Individual pursuits

Safety
Ensure that the activity space is a safe distance from walls and free of hazards (e.g., benches, equipment, basketball nets, holes, loose gravel, wet grass); remove or mark any hazards. Provide safe distances between games occurring in the same space. Remind participants to keep their heads up and to be aware of others when moving through the space.

Activity Instructions
Prior to the activity, participants look through comic books, graphic novels, and magazines noting action words such as *pow, crash, zip, bam, wow,* and *splat* that suggest a sound and a corresponding action. Record their words on poster paper.

Display the poster paper for reference throughout the activity. Participants scatter throughout the activity space. When you call out an action word from the poster, everyone travels through the space in a way that reflects the action word. Draw attention to those who are moving in creative and unique ways.

Call out two action words together so that participants have to demonstrate two movements in a sequence. Next, call out a series of four to six action words that participants must demonstrate in a sequence while moving throughout the space (each word should have its own movement).

After an appropriate amount of time, participants form groups of four or five and create a movement sequence from four to six action words. Encourage them to call out their words while performing them.

Adaptations
To decrease the challenge:
- Decrease the intensity of the movements.
- Focus on only a couple of spatial concepts (e.g., direction, pathway).
- Allow participants to respond to their own action words.

To increase the challenge:
- Require faster movements.
- Have participants change movements often.

- Place participants in pairs to perform the action words.
- Add equipment (e.g., scarves, wooden dowel, ribbons).

Self-Check Questions
- Am I moving safely in relation to the other participants?
- Do I perform movements using a variety of spatial concepts (e.g., changes in location, level, direction, pathway, and plane)?
- Do my movements demonstrate a variety of levels of force (e.g., light and strong)?

STATUES

Activity Goal
To perform a variety of locomotor movements in response to a theme while exploring planes of movement.

Fundamental Movement Skills
Agility, balance, coordination

Tactical Focus
- Move safely in relation to others.
- Travel while exploring spatial planes (e.g., frontal, horizontal, vertical, sagittal).
- Perform smooth transitions between balances.

Level
Competent

Facility
Gymnasium or outdoors

Equipment
Poster paper and markers, variety of music and audio equipment (optional)

Time
15 to 20 minutes

Activity Category

Individual pursuits

Safety

Ensure that the activity space is a safe distance from walls and free of hazards (e.g., benches, equipment, basketball nets, holes, loose gravel, wet grass); remove or mark any hazards. Remind participants to keep their heads up and to be aware of others when moving through the space.

Activity Instructions

Participants scatter throughout the activity area and hold their choice of a balance pose. Four participants at a time, as you direct, begin to move throughout the space focusing on a movement plane (e.g., frontal, horizontal, sagittal) in response to a theme you have identified. Consider using themes from another area of learning (e.g., a book recently read, bullying prevention, a science experiment), and display the theme for reference on poster paper. Participants who are moving stop and freeze at their discretion. The frozen participant closest to one who has just frozen in a pose begins moving throughout the space in response to the theme. Encourage participants to move using a variety of speeds, levels, pathways, and directions, and to freeze in different static balance poses. Point out participants who are moving or freezing in unique and creative ways. Consider using a variety of music to engage and inspire participants.

Adaptations

To decrease the challenge:

- Prior to the activity, brainstorm with participants movements they could use to reflect the theme.
- Have participants travel in pairs.
- Reduce the time spent demonstrating locomotor movements.

To increase the challenge:

- Increase the intensity of the movements.
- Have more participants actively moving in the space.
- Add equipment (e.g., ribbons, scarves, flags).

Self-Check Questions

- Am I moving safely in relation to the other participants?
- Do I explore spatial planes (e.g., frontal, horizontal, vertical, sagittal) while moving?
- Do I perform smooth transitions between movements?

BEND, STRETCH, TWIST, TURN, MEET, PART

Activity Goal

To create and travel in a sequence using a variety of body shapes in response to counts.

Fundamental Movement Skills

Agility, balance, coordination

Tactical Focus

- Move safely in relation to others.
- Travel using a variety of body shapes (e.g., wide, narrow, stretched, twisted, symmetrical, asymmetrical).
- Apply social skills that demonstrate respect for a partner.

Level

Proficient

Facility

Gymnasium or outdoors

Equipment

Poster paper, markers, variety of music and audio equipment (optional)

Time

15 to 20 minutes

Activity Category

Individual pursuits

Safety

Ensure that the activity space is a safe distance from walls and free of hazards (e.g., benches, equipment, basketball nets, holes, loose gravel, wet grass); remove or mark any hazards. Provide safe distances between partners. Remind participants to keep their heads up and to be aware of others when moving through the space.

Activity Instructions

Prior to the activity, write the words *bend, stretch, twist, turn, meet,* and *part* on poster paper for reference throughout the activity.

Participants pair up and scatter throughout the activity space. Partners perform a series of six actions to represent the words *bend, stretch, twist, turn, meet,* and *part.* Each action should take 4 counts to perform. Partners should practice a variety of movements for each word before creating routines that combine all six words. Consider using a variety of music to engage and inspire participants.

Partners perform their routines and, during the *part* sequence, find new partners. New partners then perform their original routines at the same time and on the *part* sequence, find a new partner and repeat. Choose an appropriate amount of time for this part of the activity.

Adaptations

To decrease the challenge:

- Count out loud to 4 for each movement.
- Reduce the number of movements in the sequence.
- Provide a sequence for participants to follow.

To increase the challenge:

- Have partners travel while creating symmetrical and asymmetrical body shapes.
- Extend the length of the sequence.

Self-Check Questions

- Am I moving safely in relation to the other participants?
- Am I able to travel using a variety of body shapes (e.g., wide, narrow, stretched, twisted, symmetrical, asymmetrical)?
- Do I demonstrate respect for my partner?

DANCE REPLACEMENT

Activity Goal

To work collaboratively in a group to communicate a message by performing locomotor movements in response to various genres of music.

Fundamental Movement Skills

Agility, balance, coordination, running, jumping

Tactical Focus

- Move in response to music or a theme.
- Work collaboratively with a group.
- Coordinate body parts while moving.

Level

Proficient

Facility

Gymnasium or outdoors

Equipment

Variety of music, audio equipment

Time

15 to 20 minutes

Activity Category

Individual pursuits

Safety

Ensure that the activity space is a safe distance from walls and free of hazards (e.g., benches, equipment, basketball nets, holes, loose gravel, wet grass); remove or mark any hazards. Provide safe distances between groups. Remind participants to keep their heads up and to be aware of others when dancing.

Activity Instructions

Participants form groups of three or four. Play a variety of genres of music (e.g., reggae, country, pop, rap, classical, dubstep). Group members number off. The first selects a theme (e.g., family, love, graduation, death, bullying) and dances to reflect the theme. The other group members observe for 30 to 40 seconds, or until another participant can identify the theme and calls out "Stop." The second participant replaces the first, continuing where the first dancer left off. The third participant observes and guesses the theme after 30 to 40 seconds before replacing the second participant. The activity continues until all participants have had a chance to dance.

Adaptations

To decrease the challenge:

- Provide sample movement themes for reference on poster paper.
- Have participants form pairs and perform their dances by shadowing each other.
- Reduce the time spent performing each dance.

To increase the challenge:

- Incorporate equipment into the movement sequence.
- Have pairs perform their dances in unison.
- Increase the intensity of the locomotor movements.

Self-Check Questions

- Am I moving in response to the music and theme?
- Do I demonstrate respect for the group?
- Can I coordinate body parts while moving through the activity space?

IN PURSUIT

Activity Goal

To use a variety of locomotor movements to secretly follow a peer, while traveling in response to external elements.

Fundamental Movement Skills

Agility, balance, coordination, running, jumping

Tactical Focus

- Travel in response to external stimuli.
- Travel while exploring spatial planes (e.g., frontal, horizontal, vertical, sagittal).
- Perform smooth transitions between locomotor movements.

Level

Proficient

Facility

Gymnasium or outdoors

Equipment

Variety of music, audio equipment

Time

20 to 25 minutes

Activity Category

Individual pursuits

Safety

Ensure that the activity space is a safe distance from walls and free of hazards (e.g., benches, equipment, basketball nets, holes, loose gravel, wet grass); remove or mark any hazards. Remind participants to keep their heads up and to be aware of others when moving through the space.

Activity Instructions

Participants scatter throughout the activity space performing a variety of locomotor movements. Provide verbal prompts to direct their movements (e.g., move like a tourist who has wandered into a dangerous area of town, move like a child going to a birthday party), or play a variety of music (e.g., reggae, country, pop, rap, classical, dubstep).

Next, direct participants to select someone to secretly pursue while dancing. The goal is to get as close to the person as possible without giving away that the person is being followed and then tagging them with a touch. Participants who catch the people they are pursing select another secret partner and continue dancing. Prompt participants to change whom they are pursuing often.

Adaptations

To decrease the challenge:

- Decrease the intensity of the locomotor movements.
- Play music with fewer beats per minute.
- Use music or themes familiar to participants.

To increase the challenge:

- Increase the intensity of the locomotor movements.
- Incorporate equipment into the activity.
- Do not allow participants to repeat locomotor movements.

Self-Check Questions

- Am I moving in response to the music and theme?
- Am I exploring spatial planes (e.g., frontal, horizontal, vertical, sagittal)?
- Do I perform smooth transitions between locomotor movements?

DANCE ADD-ON

Activity Goal

To work with a small group and develop and perform a locomotor sequence that demonstrates spatial awareness.

Fundamental Movement Skills

Agility, balance, coordination, running, jumping

Tactical Focus

- Perform smooth transitions between locomotor movements.
- Perform movements using a variety of spatial concepts (e.g., changes in location, level, direction, pathway, and plane).
- Demonstrate respect.

Level

Proficient

Facility

Gymnasium or outdoors

Equipment

Variety of music, audio equipment (optional)

Time

20 to 25 minutes

Activity Category

Individual pursuits

Safety

Ensure that the activity space is a safe distance from walls and free of hazards (e.g., benches, equipment, basketball nets, holes, loose gravel, wet grass); remove or mark any hazards. Provide safe distances between groups. Remind participants to keep their heads up and to be aware of others when moving through the space.

Activity Instructions

Divide participants into groups of four or five. Each group lines up single file at one end of the activity area. Participants take turns leading one locomotor movement (e.g., walk, run, skip, gallop, slide, hop) as the group moves from one end of the activity space to the other focusing on spatial concepts (e.g., changes in location, level, direction, pathway, and plane). Having added a movement for 4 to 8 counts, the leader moves to the back of the group and the next person becomes the leader. The new leader repeats the locomotor movement of the previous leader, and then adds another. Following is a sample movement sequence:

- Participant 1 performs two diagonal slides.
- Participant 2 adds a walking turn.
- Participant 3 adds two jumps.
- Participant 4 gallops for 8 counts forward and backward.
- Participant 5 runs fast for 4 counts and then slowly for 4 counts.

Once all group members have added a move, groups work together to practice and refine their sequences. Consider playing music throughout the activity.

Adaptations

To decrease the challenge:

- Decrease the intensity of the movements.
- Provide groups with a movement sequence to follow.
- Use locomotor movements that are familiar to participants.

To increase the challenge:

- Incorporate equipment into the movement sequence.
- Modify the formation or order: use the same actions, but change the formation or the order of the moves.
- Modify the timing or direction: have participants perform all actions simultaneously or in opposite directions, or echo each other's actions.

Self-Check Questions

- Do I perform smooth transitions between locomotor movements?
- Do I perform movements using a variety of spatial concepts (e.g., changes in location, level, direction, pathway, and plane)?
- Do I demonstrate respect for the group?

Running and Skipping

This chapter provides opportunities to develop and explore the fundamental movement skills of running and skipping. Jogging, sprinting, chasing, dodging, and evading are also addressed because many of the running and skipping activities involve tagging (i.e., chasing and being chased). Participants engage in a variety of partner and small-group activities with a focus on effective movement, varying speeds, and safety. They also explore the movement concepts of body (e.g., which parts of the body are moving and how), space (e.g., direction and pathway), effort (e.g., the speed and force of movements), and relationships (e.g., how the body moves in relation to others and the environment).

Although each activity highlights one fundamental movement form, individual participants may benefit from focusing on either running or skipping.

Words to Know

- **Agility.** The ability to change direction in an efficient and effective manner using a combination of balance (static and dynamic), speed, strength, and coordination.
- **Body awareness.** An awareness of the body parts that are moving, and how they are moving (e.g., shapes, actions).
- **Coordination.** The ability to use multiple parts of the body together in a controlled manner.
- **Dynamic balance.** The ability to use core strength to maintain balance and body control while moving through space (e.g., turning, rolling, balancing, landing from a jump).
- **Effort awareness.** An awareness of how the body moves (e.g., time, force, flow).
- **Relationship.** An awareness of the people, objects, or environmental features (e.g., music) one is moving with.
- **Running.** Moving quickly using the legs in such a way that both feet are simultaneously off the ground for an instant.
- **Skipping.** Moving forward using a combination of stepping and hopping on each foot.
- **Spatial awareness.** An awareness of one's own body in space (e.g., location, direction, level, pathway, plane, extensions).

Running Transferable Skills

Upper-Body Position	Lower-Body Position
1. Center the head between the shoulders and look ahead.	1. Lift the knees high.
2. Relax the jaw and neck.	2. Contact the ground with a midfoot or heel strike under the body's center of gravity.
3. Lean slightly forward.	3. Push off the ground with the ball of the foot.
4. Keep the shoulders relaxed and parallel to the ground.	
5. Lightly cup the hands.	
6. Bend the elbows at approximately 90 degrees.	
7. Swing the arms backward and forward from the shoulders. Don't let them cross the midline of the body.	
8. Move the arms and legs in opposition.	

Running learning cues: Keep the hands relaxed, bend the elbows, swing forward and back, keep a tall body, run softly.

Skipping Transferable Skills

Upper-Body Position	Lower-Body Position
1. Center the head between the shoulders and look ahead.	1. Step forward and then hop on the same foot.
2. Relax the jaw and neck.	2. Lift the other knee high before stepping forward and hopping on that foot.
3. Lean slightly forward.	
4. Keep the shoulders relaxed and parallel to the ground.	3. Contact the ground with the midfoot under the body's center of gravity.
5. Lightly cup the hands.	
6. Bend elbows at approximately 90 degrees.	4. Push off the ground with the ball of the foot.
7. Swing the arms backward and forward from the shoulders. Don't let them cross the midline of the body.	
8. Move the arms and legs in opposition.	

Skipping learning cues: Step forward and hop on the same foot, repeat with the other foot, push off the ground while lifting the knee up.

Where's the Physical Literacy?

Running and skipping are important in many games, dances, sports, and everyday activities. In these activities, participants develop the confidence and competence to run and skip safely and effectively and then transfer that knowledge to other contexts, including sustained running or skipping and speed activities, evading opponents (e.g., in tag games), performing creative movement sequences, and running for fun and fitness with others.

While running, participants explore the movement principles of applied impulse-causing momentum (e.g., the greater the force produced from the drive off the back leg, the greater the forward acceleration), summation of joints (e.g., the production of maximal force requires the use of all possible joints), and direction of force (e.g., all body movement should be lateral and forward in the direction of the run).

While skipping, participants explore the law of reaction/force (e.g., force should be applied upward in the hop action to allow the opposite leg to swing forward freely) as well as balance (e.g., shifting weight from one foot to the other over a narrow base of support).

Educator Check and Reflect

- Consider modifying distance and speed during some running games to meet the needs of participants at different ability levels.
- Provide the option to walk, as appropriate.
- Consider providing opportunities for participants to track and reflect on their progress regarding distance and speed.
- Use cones to mark distances for participants to choose from.
- Discuss pacing tips and strategies with participants (e.g., sing your favorite song in your head and keep pace with the beat, count your steps, ask yourself *Can I hold this pace for three more minutes?*).

CAT IN A TREE

Activity Goal

To skip safely throughout the activity space in relation to others.

Fundamental Movement Skills

Skipping, balance

Tactical Focus

Apply appropriate movement skills.

Level

Beginning

Facility

Gymnasium or outdoors

Equipment

None

Time

10 to 15 minutes

Activity Category

Individual pursuits

Safety

Ensure that indoor and outdoor activity spaces are a safe distance from walls and free of hazards (e.g., benches, equipment, basketball nets, holes, loose gravel, wet grass); remove or mark any hazards. Remind participants to keep their heads up and to be aware of others when moving through the space.

Activity Instructions

Divide participants into groups of three. Two participants create a tree by standing side by side in tree pose (balancing on one leg with the foot of the other leg firmly against the shin of the standing leg); they hold hands (just two) and lift those hands high. The third participant crouches under the partners' arms (i.e., is the cat in the tree).

On your signal, the cat skips around the activity area, moving in a variety of pathways and directions around the trees. When you call out "Dog's coming," the cats find the closest tree and crouch there. Only one cat is allowed in a tree at a time. Switch cats and trees often.

Adaptations

To decrease the challenge:

- Allow the trees to balance on two feet.
- Permit multiple cats to hide in the same tree.
- Reduce the time spent skipping.

To increase the challenge:

- Reduce the number of trees available to hide in.
- Add dogs who try to tag the cats before they are safely in trees.
- Increase the size of the activity area.

Self-Check Questions

- Am I moving safely in relation to the other participants?
- Do my arms swing freely at my sides?
- Can I skip quickly? Can I change direction?

AT THE RACE TRACK

Activity Goal

To run safely around the activity space in relation to others.

Fundamental Movement Skill

Running

Tactical Focus

Apply appropriate movement skills.

Level

Beginning

Facility

Gymnasium or outdoors

Equipment

None

Time

10 to 15 minutes

Activity Category

Individual pursuits

Safety

Ensure that indoor and outdoor activity spaces are a safe distance from walls and free of hazards (e.g., benches, equipment, basketball nets, holes, loose gravel, wet grass); remove or mark any hazards. Remind participants to keep their heads up and to be aware of others when running.

Activity Instructions

Participants form a large circle, and each is assigned a type of vehicle (e.g. car, bus, motorcycle). When you call out a vehicle, participants assigned that vehicle race around the circle clockwise and then back to their garages (i.e., original spaces). If space permits, consider calling out "Rush hour," at which point all participants race around the circle to their garages.

Adaptations

To decrease the challenge:

- Have participants work with a partner.
- Call only one or two vehicles to reduce the number of participants running at a time.

To increase the challenge:

- Increase the size of the circle.
- Add one participant in the center who joins each round and attempts to take other vehicles' garages by racing them around the circle.

Self-Check Questions

- Am I moving safely in relation to the other participants?
- Do I move my arms opposite to my legs?
- Do I look ahead while I'm running?

SHADOW TAG

Activity Goal

To avoid having one's shadow tagged by skipping.

Fundamental Movement Skill

Skipping

Tactical Focus

- Apply appropriate movement skills (e.g., step-hop smoothly, land on toes) to move around safely.
- Demonstrate appropriate strategies to avoid being tagged.

Level

Beginning

Facility

Outdoors

Equipment

2 or 3 markers for taggers (e.g., pinnies, gloves, fake flower leis)

Time

10 to 15 minutes

Activity Category

Individual pursuits

Safety

Ensure that the activity space is free of hazards (e.g., loose gravel, wet grass); remove or mark any hazards. Remind participants to keep their heads up and to be aware of others when moving through the space.

Activity Instructions

Choose two or three participants to be taggers and identify them with markers (pinnies, gloves, fake flower leis). Participants skip around the activity area, and taggers attempt to tag their shadows by stepping on them. Tagged participants must freeze until other participants skip in a circle around them, at which point they may rejoin the game. Change taggers often.

Adaptations

To decrease the challenge:

- Increase the size of the activity space.
- Reduce the number of taggers.
- Require taggers to walk.
- Allow taggers to use implements to help them tag (e.g., pool noodles).

To increase the challenge:

- Decrease the size of the activity space.
- Increase the number of taggers.

Self-Check Questions

- Is my step-hop pattern smooth and coordinated?
- Do I use my arms in the hopping action?
- Do I land on my toes?

Activity Goal

To run quickly with teammates while trying to tag or avoid getting tagged by an alien.

Fundamental Movement Skill

Running

Tactical Focus

- Apply appropriate movement skills (e.g., hold head up, look ahead, move arms and legs in opposition) to move around safely.
- Work collaboratively and apply problem-solving skills with teammates to protect the captain.

Level

Exploring

Facility

Gymnasium or outdoors

Equipment

None

Time

15 to 20 minutes

Activity Category

Individual pursuits

Safety

Ensure that indoor and outdoor activity spaces are a safe distance from walls and free of hazards (e.g., benches, equipment, basketball nets, holes, loose gravel, wet grass); remove or mark any hazards. Remind participants to keep their heads up and to be aware of others when moving through the space.

Activity Instructions

Participants form groups of four. Three group members hold hands in a circle, and the fourth member is outside the circle (i.e., the alien). One member in the circle is the captain of the spaceship; the other two are astronauts. The alien tries to capture the captain by running around the circle (not reaching through), while the astronauts try to protect the captain by moving around quickly while not releasing their hands. Have group members change roles often.

Adaptations

To decrease the challenge:

- Have more astronauts in each group.
- Require that aliens walk.
- Allow aliens to use implements to help them tag captains (e.g., pool noodles).

To increase the challenge:

- Decrease the number of astronauts.
- Increase the number of aliens.

Self-Check Questions

- Am I moving safely in relation to the other participants?
- Do I lean slightly forward?
- Do my arms move in opposition to my legs?
- Do I look ahead while running?

10-METER DASH

Activity Goal

To run at various speeds and move safely around obstacles.

Fundamental Movement Skill

Running

Tactical Focus

- Apply appropriate movement skills (e.g., hold head up, look ahead, move arms opposite to legs) to move around safely.
- Develop and apply appropriate strategies to maintain speed (e.g., lean in the direction of the run, reduce lateral movements).

Level

Exploring

Facility

Outdoors

Equipment

25 to 30 cones

Time

15 to 20 minutes

Activity Category

Individual pursuits

Safety

Ensure that the activity space is free of hazards (e.g., loose gravel, wet grass); remove or mark any hazards. Remind participants to keep their heads up and to be aware of others when moving through the space.

Activity Instructions

Prior to the activity, set up five to six sets of five cones 10 meters apart in the activity space.

Working in small groups of four to six, participants line up in line with the first set of cones. On your signal (e.g., whistle, calling "Go"), the first participant in each group runs as fast as possible (sprints) to the first cone, runs slowly (recovers) to the second cone, sprints to the third cone, and so on, alternating sprinting and recovering until the final cone. At the final cone, participants jog slowly back to the starting position. The next participant in each group begins when the previous participant reaches the first cone.

Adaptations

To decrease the challenge:

- Reduce the distance between the cones.
- Reduce the number of cones.
- Increase the distance between the recovery cones.
- Have participants alternate between running and walking between the cones.

To increase the challenge:

- Increase the distance between the sprinting cones.
- Increase the number of cones.
- Add obstacles for participants to run around.

Self-Check Questions

- Am I moving safely in relation to the other participants?
- Do my arms and legs move in opposition?
- Do I run tall with my head up?

IF, YOU RUN

Activity Goal

To run safely around a circle in relation to others.

Fundamental Movement Skill

Running

Tactical Focus

Apply appropriate movement skills (e.g., hold head up, look ahead, move arms and legs in opposition) to move around safely.

Level

Exploring

Facility

Gymnasium or outdoors

Equipment

None

Time

15 to 20 minutes

Activity Category

Individual pursuits

Safety

Ensure that indoor and outdoor activity spaces are a safe distance from walls and free of hazards (e.g., benches, equipment, basketball nets, holes, loose gravel, wet grass); remove or mark any hazards. Remind participants to keep their heads up and to be aware of others when running around the circle.

Activity Instructions

Participants form a large circle and jog in place. One person is in the center and calls out a question (e.g., Are you wearing blue? Did you have cereal for breakfast? Do you know how to ice skate?). Participants who answer yes must leave their spots and run around the circle before returning to their spots. The questioner joins the group running around the circle and attempts to take someone's place in the circle. If the questioner succeeds, the misplaced person becomes the questioner. Change questioners often.

Adaptations

To decrease the challenge:

- Decrease the size of the circle.
- Have participants run with a partner.
- Require that participants walk around the circle.

To increase the challenge:

- Have more than one participant in the center working together as the questioner.
- Increase the size of the circle.

Self-Check Questions

- Do I keep my head up?
- Do I move my arms and legs in opposition?
- Are my arms bent and swinging back and forth?

COUCH POTATO TAG

Activity Goal

To run safely throughout the activity space while trying to tag or avoid getting tagged.

Fundamental Movement Skill

Running

Tactical Focus

- Apply appropriate movement skills (e.g., look ahead, lean slightly forward, lift the knees) to move around safely.
- Demonstrate appropriate strategies to avoid being tagged.

Level

Exploring

Facility

Gymnasium or outdoors

Equipment

None

Time

10 to 15 minutes

Activity Category

Individual pursuits

Safety

Ensure that indoor and outdoor activity spaces are a safe distance from walls and free of hazards (e.g., benches, equipment, basketball nets, holes, loose gravel, wet grass); remove or mark any hazards. Remind participants to keep their heads up and to be aware of others when moving through the space.

Activity Instructions

One participant is designated as the tagger. Tagged players must freeze in a squat to signify sitting on a couch watching TV or playing video games. To be freed, tagged players must be joined by another participant who performs a physical task five times with them (e.g., jumping jack, jogging in place, tuck jump). Be sure to change taggers often.

Adaptations

To decrease the challenge:

- Increase the size of the activity space.
- Require that taggers walk while others run.
- Permit taggers to use an implement to help them tag (e.g., a pool noodle).

To increase the challenge:

- Increase the intensity of the physical tasks to reenter the game.
- Decrease the size of the activity space.

Self-Check Questions

- Do I hold my head up and look ahead while running?
- Do I lean slightly forward?
- Do I bend my arms at the elbows, swinging them back and forth from my shoulders?

RELAY RUN

Activity Goal

To run quickly and safely in relation to teammates and opponents.

Fundamental Movement Skill

Running

Tactical Focus

- Apply appropriate movement skills (e.g., look ahead, lean slightly forward, lift the knees) to move around safely.
- Develop and apply appropriate strategies to maintain speed (e.g., push off the ground with the back leg to accelerate).

Level

Exploring

Facility

Gymnasium or outdoors

Equipment

None

Time

15 to 20 minutes

Activity Category

Individual pursuits

Safety

Ensure that indoor and outdoor activity spaces are a safe distance from walls and free of hazards (e.g., benches, equipment, basketball nets, holes, loose gravel, wet grass); remove or mark any hazards. Remind participants to keep their heads up and to be aware of others when running.

Activity Instructions

Divide participants into groups of four. Two people from each group line up across the activity space from their partners. Group members number off and pair up (players 1 and 3 stand together, and players 2 and 4 stand together). On your signal (e.g., whistle, clap hands, call out "Go"), player 1 runs across the activity space to high-five player 2 and stays there. Next, player 2 runs to high-five player 3 at the starting line and stays there while player 3 runs to high-five player 4. Player 3 stays there while player 4 runs to high-five player 1. Waiting players can run in place or perform their favorite fitness tasks (e.g., jumping jack, squat, calf raise). Continue the relay until all players have returned to their original places.

Adaptations

To decrease the challenge:

- Reduce the distance between teammates.
- Participants use different types of locomotor movements.

To increase the challenge:

- Increase the distance between teammates.
- Vary the setup (e.g., players must run through an obstacle course or in specific movement pathways).

Self-Check Questions

- Do I lean slightly forward while running?
- Do I push off the balls of my feet while running?
- Are my elbows bent while running?

SPEEDY LEADER

Activity Goal

To mirror the speed of a partner while running around the activity space.

Fundamental Movement Skill

Running

Tactical Focus

- Apply appropriate movement skills (e.g., look ahead, lean slightly forward, lift the knees) to move around safely.
- Develop and apply appropriate strategies to maintain speed (e.g., push off the ground with the back leg to accelerate).
- Work collaboratively with a partner to change speeds in unison.

Level

Competent

Facility

Outdoors

Equipment

None

Time

15 to 20 minutes

Activity Category

Individual pursuits

Safety

Ensure that the activity space is free of hazards (e.g., loose gravel, wet grass); remove or mark any hazards. Remind participants to keep their heads up and to be aware of others when moving through the space.

Activity Instructions

Participants work in pairs and stand opposite each other across the activity area. One partner is the leader and begins to jog slowly around the activity area, randomly speeding up to a sprint and slowing down. The partner mirrors the leader, adjusting speed to remain across the activity area from the leader.

Adaptations

To decrease the challenge:

- Decrease the intensity of the run.
- Decrease the size of the activity space.

To increase the challenge:

- Increase the intensity of the run.
- Increase the size of the activity space.
- Have participants track the number of laps they perform within a designated time and try to beat it each round.

Self-Check Questions

- Am I moving safely in relation to the other participants?
- Am I able to monitor how hard I am working throughout the activity?
- Do the balls of my feet contact the ground first when I'm running fast?

Activity Goal

To move at assigned speeds while trying to tag or avoid getting tagged.

Fundamental Movement Skill

Skipping

Tactical Focus

- Apply appropriate movement skills (e.g., step-hop smoothly, land on toes) to move around safely.
- Demonstrate appropriate strategies to avoid being tagged.

Level

Competent

Facility

Gymnasium or outdoors

Equipment

2 or 3 markers for taggers (e.g., pinnies, gloves, fake flower leis)

Time

10 to 15 minutes

Activity Category

Individual pursuits

Safety

Ensure that indoor and outdoor activity spaces are a safe distance from walls and free of hazards (e.g., benches, equipment, basketball nets, holes, loose gravel, wet grass); remove or mark any hazards. Remind participants to keep their heads up and to be aware of others when moving through the space.

Activity Instructions

Choose two or three participants to be taggers and identify them with markers (e.g., pinnies, gloves, fake flower leis). Participants skip around the activity area. Call out "snails" or "deer". On the signal "snails", both participants and taggers skip slowly. On the signal "deer", both participants and taggers skip quickly. Tagged players become taggers and take possession of a marker.

Adaptations

To decrease the challenge:

- Have taggers walk.
- Decrease the number of taggers.
- Give taggers implements to extend their reach (e.g., pool noodles).

To increase the challenge:

- Increase the number of taggers.
- Decrease the size of the playing area.

Self-Check Questions

- Do I step forward and hop on the same foot?
- Do I lift my knees high?
- Do I land on my toes?

SMOOTHIE TAG

Activity Goal

To move safely around the activity area while trying to tag or avoid getting tagged.

Fundamental Movement Skill

Skipping

Tactical Focus

- Apply appropriate movement skills (e.g., step-hop smoothly, land on toes) to move around safely.
- Demonstrate appropriate strategies to avoid being tagged.

Level

Competent

Facility

Gymnasium or outdoors

Equipment

2 or 3 markers for taggers (e.g., pinnies, gloves, fake flower leis)

Activity Category

Individual pursuits

Safety

Ensure that indoor and outdoor activity spaces are a safe distance from walls and free of hazards (e.g., benches, equipment, basketball nets, holes, loose gravel, wet grass); remove or mark any hazards. Remind participants to keep their heads up and to be aware of others when moving through the space.

Activity Instructions

Designate two or three participants to be taggers who are gathering ingredients to make everyone a post-workout smoothie. Taggers stand in the middle of the activity space. The other participants, each assigned to be a smoothie ingredient (e.g., strawberries, bananas, mangos, raspberries), stand at one end of the activity area. The smoothie makers collectively call out one ingredient at a time, and those identified participants skip to the other side of the activity area while trying to avoid being tagged. Tagged participants switch roles with the smoothie makers who tagged them.

Adaptations

To decrease the challenge:

- Have taggers walk.
- Decrease the number of taggers.
- Allow taggers to use an implement to extend their reach (e.g., a pool noodle).

To increase the challenge:

- Increase the number of taggers.
- Decrease the size of the playing area.
- Designate a time limit for running to the other side of the playing area.

Self-Check Questions

- Am I moving safely in relation to the other participants?
- Do I step forward and hop on the same foot?
- Do I land on my toes?

RUN ACROSS THE WORLD

Activity Goal

To run as much as required to virtually travel to a destination.

Fundamental Movement Skill

Running

Tactical Focus

- Demonstrate appropriate movement skills (e.g., good length stride, even rhythm and flight phase).
- Develop and apply appropriate strategies to maintain speed (e.g., push off the ground with the back leg to accelerate).

Level

Competent

Facility

Outdoors

Equipment

Map of destinations

Time

25 to 30 minutes

Activity Category

Individual pursuits

Safety

Ensure that the outdoor activity space is free of hazards (e.g., loose gravel, wet grass). Remind participants to keep their heads up and to be aware of others when moving through the space.

Activity Instructions

Working as a large group, participants choose destinations to reach by running the equivalent distance locally. One lap of the activity area could equal 1 kilometer or 1 mile. Participants run laps of the activity area at their own pace and record the distances they complete on their map. Consider linking the locations to other areas of study or to socially or culturally relevant sites. Locate participants' destinations on a map and display it for the duration of the activity. Consider recording the group's accumulated distance and plotting it on an enlarged map. This activity is ongoing and can occur over several weeks or classes, as appropriate.

Adaptations

To decrease the challenge:

- Decrease the intensity of the run.
- Decrease the size of the activity area.
- Allow participants to walk and run.

To increase the challenge:

- Increase the size of the activity area.
- Modify the terrain to include hills and obstacles.
- Have participants track the time they take to complete each lap and try to beat it each round.

Self-Check Questions

- Does my stride have an even rhythm?
- Do I extend my supporting leg fully?
- Are my arms bent and swinging back and forth in opposition to my legs?

EVEN STEVEN

Activity Goal

To maintain a pace while running around a designated activity area.

Fundamental Movement Skill

Running

Tactical Focus

- Understand personal areas of strength and those in need of improvement.
- Develop and apply appropriate strategies to maintain a running pace (e.g., perceived exertion).

Level

Proficient

Facility

Gymnasium or outdoors

Equipment

3 stopwatches per group

Time

20 to 25 minutes

Activity Category

Individual pursuits

Safety

Ensure that indoor and outdoor activity spaces are a safe distance from walls and free of hazards (e.g., benches, equipment, basketball nets, holes, loose gravel, wet grass); remove or mark any hazards. Provide safe distances between groups in the same space. Remind participants to keep their heads up and to be aware of others when moving through the space.

Activity Instructions

Participants form groups of six. Three participants are timers and are spread out across the activity area an equal distance apart. On your signal, the timers start their watches; the remaining three participants run laps of the activity area past the timers. As the runners pass them, the timers call out the times on their watches. Runners try to pace themselves so that they run each section in the same amount of time. After three laps, runners switch places with timers, and the activity repeats. After the first round, challenge participants to run the same distance faster and then slower, but always maintaining an even pace.

Adaptations

To decrease the challenge:

- Decrease the intensity of the run.
- Decrease the size of the activity area.
- Do not provide timers; have participants run based on personal feel (e.g., perceived exertion).

To increase the challenge:

- Increase the size of the activity area.
- Modify the terrain to include hills and obstacles.
- Give each runner a suggested pace and time in which to complete each lap.

Self-Check Questions

- Do I bend my arms at the elbows and swing my arms back and forth from my shoulders?
- Do I move my arms and legs in opposition?
- Do I push off with the balls of my feet?
- As I increase my running speed, do I lean, and does my arm action increase?

TAG TEAM

Activity Goal

To tag or avoid being tagged in a small-group skipping game.

Fundamental Movement Skill

Skipping

Tactical Focus

- Apply appropriate movement skills (e.g., step-hop smoothly, land on toes) to move around safely.
- Demonstrate appropriate strategies to avoid being tagged.

Level

Proficient

Facility

Gymnasium or outdoors

Equipment

None

Time

10 to 15 minutes

Activity Category

Individual pursuits

Safety

Ensure that indoor and outdoor activity spaces are a safe distance from walls and free of hazards (e.g., benches, equipment, basketball nets, holes, loose gravel, wet grass); remove or mark any hazards. Provide safe distances between groups in the same space. Remind participants to keep their heads up and to be aware of others when moving through the space.

Activity Instructions

Participants form groups of three and number off. When you call out a number, the players with that number skip away from their groups as quickly as possible. Count to 4 (or choose another number), after which the two remaining players skip to chase and attempt to tag the first players. Once tagged, or after a specific amount of time, the three participants return to their starting positions. Be sure to call out all numbers to change the taggers and skippers often.

Adaptations

To decrease the challenge:

- Have taggers walk.
- Decrease the number of taggers.
- Allow taggers to use an implement to extend their reach (e.g., a pool noodle).

To increase the challenge:

- Increase the number of taggers.
- Decrease the size of the playing area.

Self-Check Questions

- Do I understand where to skip to avoid being tagged?
- Is my step–hop pattern smooth and coordinated?
- Do I use my arms in the hopping action, and are they coordinated throughout the movement?
- Do I land on my toes?

Activity Goal

To take turns leading the pace as well as holding the pace for others during a two-minute sprinting interval.

Fundamental Movement Skill

Running

Tactical Focus

- Demonstrate appropriate movement skills (e.g., good length stride, even rhythm and flight phase) to move around safely.
- Develop and apply appropriate strategies to maintain speed (e.g., push off the ground with the back leg to accelerate).

Level

Proficient

Facility

Outdoors

Equipment

1 stopwatch per group

Time

15 to 20 minutes

Activity Category

Individual pursuits

Safety

Ensure that indoor and outdoor activity spaces are a safe distance from walls and free of hazards (e.g., benches, equipment, basketball nets, holes, loose gravel, wet grass); remove or mark any hazards. Provide safe distances between groups in the same space. Remind participants to keep their heads up and to be aware of others when running.

Activity Instructions

Participants form groups of four or five. One participant in the group will have a stopwatch and be the timer while actively participating in the task. Groups run in single file, with each member of the group taking a turn leading. Group leaders set the pace for the group during a two-minute sprint followed by a two-minute recovery. After the recovery, the group leader moves to the end of the line and the next leader takes a turn. Participants at the back must work to match the pace of the leader to keep the group together.

Adaptations

To decrease the challenge:

- Decrease the total time spent running.
- Increase the recovery time.
- Reduce the time spent sprinting.

To increase the challenge:

- Increase the time spent sprinting.
- Create larger groups.
- Have participants track the distances they cover during each lap and try to beat them each round.

Self-Check Questions

- Am I moving in relation to the other runners?
- Am I able to monitor how hard I am working throughout the task?
- Do the balls of my feet contact the ground first when I'm running fast?

CHAPTER **6**

Throwing and Catching

This chapter focuses on the fundamental movement skills of throwing and catching. Participants explore throwing a variety of objects both underhand and overhand while applying the movement concept of effort awareness (e.g., time and force). Participants also explore the complementary skill of catching various objects in game situations while working in pairs and small groups. These two skills are often practiced together; however, the lack of ability in one skill should not affect the practice and development of the other.

Most activities in this chapter permit participants to choose their own objects and targets to ensure an optimal level of challenge. Object choices include type, size, and color; target choices involve size and proximity to the thrower.

Words to Know

- **Catching.** Obtaining an object in flight with the hands, arms, or an implement.
- **Throwing overhand.** Sending an object with controlled force through the air with the hand positioned above the shoulder.
- **Throwing underhand.** Sending an object with controlled force through the air with the hand positioned below the shoulder.

Underhand Throwing Transferable Skills

Preparation	Execution	Follow-Through
1. Adopt an athletic stance (e.g., strong base of support, balanced). 2. Lengthen the throwing arm down and back behind the body. 3. Keep the eyes on the target.	1. Step forward onto the leg opposite the throwing arm. 2. Move the body weight forward while rotating the body to face the target. 3. Swing the arm down alongside the body. 4. Release the object toward the target.	1. End with the weight on the opposite foot. 2. Point the throwing arm toward the target. 3. Readopt the athletic stance (e.g., strong base of support, balanced) to be in position to perform the next movement.

Underhand throwing learning cues: Keep the eyes on the target, swing the arm straight back, step forward on the foot opposite the throwing arm, swing the arm forward, follow through toward the target.

Overhand Throwing Transferable Skills

Preparation	Execution	Follow-Through
1. Adopt an athletic stance (e.g., strong base of support, balanced). 2. Grip the object with the fingers, not the palm. 3. Face sideways with the trunk rotated back toward the throwing arm side of the body. 4. Lengthen the throwing arm down and back behind the body. 5. Keep the eyes on the target.	1. Step forward with the leg opposite the throwing arm. 2. Move the body weight forward while rotating the body to face the target, with the nonthrowing arm pointed in the direction of the throw. 3. Bend the throwing arm to bring the object up from behind and then above the ear. 4. Drop the nonthrowing arm down and back. 5. Release the object toward the target.	1. End with the weight on the opposite foot. 2. Point the throwing arm toward the target, then follow through down and across the body. 3. Readopt the athletic stance (e.g., strong base of support, balanced) to be in position to perform the next movement.

Overhand throwing learning cues: Keep the eyes on the target, put the weight on the rear foot, step forward on the foot opposite the throwing arm, follow through toward the target.

Catching Transferable Skills

Preparation	Execution	Follow-Through
1. Adopt an athletic stance (e.g., strong base of support, balanced). 2. Provide a target for the sender (i.e., hands out and ready to catch). 3. Keep the body between the object and the defender. 4. Keep the eyes on the path of the object until received.	1. Reach out to meet the object. 2. Receive the object with the appropriate implement (e.g., hands, feet, scoop).	1. Absorb the force of the object. 2. Bring the object toward the body. 3. Readopt the athletic stance (e.g., strong base of support, balanced) with the object in position to perform the next movement.

Catching learning cues: Move the body into the path of the object, keep the eyes on the object, present a large surface area for catching, absorb the object into the body.

Where's the Physical Literacy?

Although they are complementary, throwing and catching are unique fundamental movement skills. Throwing provides an opportunity to propel an object toward a target (person or object). While throwing, participants explore the movement concept of effort awareness as they play with time (e.g., slow, medium, fast) and force (e.g., light, strong). Catching provides an opportunity to explore eye–hand coordination while tracking an object from a thrower into the receiving part of the body or object. People who are confident about and competent in throwing and catching can explore a variety of physical activities, including sports and individual pursuits.

Educator Check and Reflect

- Instruct participants regarding safe use of equipment.
- Provide a variety of equipment for participants and groups to choose from when throwing and catching.
- Ensure that no one is located between the target and the thrower.
- Place catchers a safe distance behind home plate. They should not be responsible for catching the pitch, but simply be used to retrieve the ball. The catcher must wear a mask and other protective gear as directed by facility policy.
- Establish sliding rules based on facility policy (e.g., no sliding).
- Inspect outdoor areas for hazards (e.g., glass, rocks, holes).
- To reduce wait time and maximize physical activity, ensure that activities taking place at the same time are a safe distance apart.

ROLLED OVER

Activity Goal

To accurately roll objects toward targets.

Fundamental Movement Skill

Throwing underhand

Tactical Focus

Offense: Determine an appropriate distance from which to throw an object.

Level

Beginning

Facility

Gymnasium or outdoors

Equipment

30 to 40 targets (e.g., bowling pins, empty water bottles, empty detergent jugs, paper towel rolls), 15 to 20 balls (various sizes)

Time

15 to 20 minutes

Activity Category

Target

Safety

Ensure that indoor and outdoor activity spaces are a safe distance from walls and free of hazards (e.g., benches, equipment, basketball nets, holes, loose gravel, wet grass); remove or mark any hazards. Provide safe distances between groups. Remind participants to keep their heads up and to be aware of others.

Activity Instructions

Groups of two to four select four or five objects to be used as targets, as well as a ball. Group members determine a distance from the target that will provide an optimal challenge. One participant stands at the targets and tells the others the order in which to hit the targets. The first member rolls the ball toward the designated target. Participants alternate turns until all targets have been hit. Consider having groups count the number of rolls they take to knock the targets down.

Adaptations

To decrease the challenge:

- Decrease the distance between the roll line and the targets.
- Have groups roll larger objects.
- Have groups use a scooter board like a curling stone to hit the targets.

To increase the challenge:

- Increase the distance between the roll line and the targets.
- Keep individual scores instead of team scores.
- Require that the thrower knock down two targets during one roll.
- Assign varying points to targets (i.e., more challenging targets earn more points).

Self-Check Questions

- Am I able to control the spin of the ball during my roll?
- Can I apply the required amount of force for the ball to reach the designated target?
- Do I follow through toward the designated target after releasing the ball?

TARGET TIP-OVER

Activity Goal

To collect points by knocking down as many balls as possible and landing a ball in a hoop.

Fundamental Movement Skill

Throwing underhand

Tactical Focus

Offense: Determine an appropriate distance from which to throw an object.

Level

Beginning

Facility

Gymnasium or outdoors

Equipment

6 to 8 soft skin balls (various sizes), 6 to 8 hula hoops, 6 to 8 cones, 25 to 30 objects (e.g., beanbags, rubber chickens, balls, stuffed animals, hockey pucks)

Time

15 to 20 minutes

Activity Category

Target

Safety

Ensure that indoor and outdoor activity spaces are a safe distance from walls and free of hazards (e.g., benches, equipment, basketball nets, holes, loose gravel, wet grass); remove or mark any hazards. Provide safe distances between groups. Remind participants to keep their heads up and to be aware of others when throwing.

Activity Instructions

Each group of three or four creates a target by placing a cone inside a hula hoop and balancing a ball on the cone. Standing at a distance of optimal challenge from the target, participants take turns throwing selected objects underhand at the target. Groups score 1 point for each object that lands in the hoop and 2 points for knocking the ball off the cone.

Adaptations

To decrease the challenge:

- Decrease the distance between the throwing line and the target.
- Remove the target ball, or both target ball and cone.
- Provide multiple targets.
- Allow groups to choose an object to place on the cone.

To increase the challenge:

- Increase the distance from the throwing line to the target.

- Have throwers use an implement (e.g., scoop, hockey stick, ringette stick, pool noodle).
- Require that throwers use their nondominant hands.

Self-Check Questions

- Can I apply the required amount of force to get the object to the target?
- Do I follow through toward the target when I release the object?
- Do I know my own strength and throw the right object to hit the target?

ON THE RUN

Activity Goal

To complete as many runs as possible.

Fundamental Movement Skills

Throwing underhand, catching, running

Tactical Focus

- Offense: Move quickly to score runs.
- Defense: Stop runs from scoring.

Level

Beginning

Facility

Gymnasium or outdoors

Equipment

6 to 8 soft skin balls (various sizes) or beanbags (1 per group)

Time

20 to 25 minutes

Activity Category

Striking/fielding

Safety

Ensure that indoor and outdoor activity spaces are a safe distance from walls and free of hazards (e.g., benches, equipment, basketball nets, holes, loose gravel, wet grass); remove or mark any hazards. Provide safe distances between groups. Remind participants to keep their heads up and to be aware of others when running.

Activity Instructions

Participants form groups of five and select one object to throw. Four participants stand in a square and throw the object underhand to each other around the square twice, in a pattern of their choice. The fifth participant runs around the square as many times as possible while the others are throwing, counting the number of circuits completed in the time it takes the four participants to complete their passes. Change runners often.

Adaptations

To decrease the challenge:

- Decrease the distance between the throwers.
- Decrease the number of throwers.
- Allow participants to throw with both hands or roll the object.
- Use an object that is easier to throw and catch (e.g., rubber chicken, foam ring).

To increase the challenge:

- Increase the distance between the throwers.
- Modify the form of locomotion used by the runner.
- Provide smaller or unfamiliar objects.

Self-Check Questions

- Do I apply the required amount of force to send the object to my group mates?
- Do I follow through toward my group mates when I release the object?
- Do I watch the object until it lands in my hands?
- Do I catch the object and hug it to my body?

Activity Goal

To complete one run without being tagged.

Fundamental Movement Skills

Throwing underhand, catching

Tactical Focus

- Offense: Move quickly to score runs.
- Defense: Stop runs from scoring.

Level

Beginning

Facility

Gymnasium or outdoors

Equipment

6 to 8 objects (e.g., soft skin balls of various sizes, discs, footballs)

Time

20 to 25 minutes

Activity Category

Striking/fielding

Safety

Ensure that indoor and outdoor activity spaces are a safe distance from walls and free of hazards (e.g., benches, equipment, basketball nets, holes, loose gravel, wet grass); remove or mark any hazards. Provide safe distances between groups. Remind participants to keep their heads up and to be aware of objects being thrown and others running around the activity space.

Activity Instructions

Participants form groups of five or six and select one object to throw. Four or five group members form a circle, and one stands in the middle with the object. The thrower tosses the object to someone in the circle while calling out a physical task (e.g., jumping jack, squat, heel dig). Group members who did not catch the object perform the physical task while the thrower runs out of the circle and attempts to complete one lap and reach the middle before the person who caught the object can place the object in the middle and chase and tag the thrower. A thrower who is not tagged gets to throw again, and the catcher returns to the circle. Participants cannot throw to the same person twice in a row. Change runners often.

Adaptations

To decrease the challenge:

- Decrease the size of the circle.
- Allow participants to select the object.
- Permit participants to throw with both hands or roll the object.
- Have participants start off with rolling and progress to throwing.

To increase the challenge:

- Increase the size of the circle.
- Increase the number of objects thrown.
- Require that throwers use their nondominant hands.

Self-Check Questions

- Do I apply the amount of force required for the throw?
- Do I step forward and swing my throwing arm back during the throw?
- Do I reach out for the object when catching?
- Do I run quickly to tag the thrower?

DISC LANDING

Activity Goal

To throw a disc to hit or land on a target.

Fundamental Movement Skill

Throwing backhand

Tactical Focus

Offense: Determine an appropriate distance from which to throw an object, avoid obstacles.

Level

Exploring

Facility

Gymnasium or outdoors

Equipment

5 to 7 discs, 10 to 14 cones

Time

20 to 25 minutes

Activity Category

Target

Safety

Ensure that indoor and outdoor activity spaces are a safe distance from walls and free of hazards (e.g., benches, equipment, basketball nets, holes, loose gravel, wet grass); remove or mark any hazards. Provide safe distances between games occurring in the same space. Remind participants to keep their heads up and to be aware of discs being thrown.

Activity Instructions

Set up multiple games by placing two cones at an optimal distance apart (e.g., 10 to 15 ft, or 3 to 4.5 m), and having teams of three or four stand behind each cone. Teams take turns attempting to land a disc on the opposing team's cone. Hitting a cone earns 3 points; landing a disc on a cone earns 5 points. The winning score is 21 points.

Adaptations

To decrease the challenge:

- Decrease the distance between the cones.
- Award points for being closest to the cone.
- Modify the throwing objects (e.g., larger discs, rings).
- Increase the size of the target (e.g., hula hoops).

To increase the challenge:

- Increase the distance between the cones.
- Keep individual scores instead of team scores.
- Have players use their nondominant hands.

Self-Check Questions

- Before throwing, do I line the disc up with the target?
- Do apply the required amount of force to land the disc on the target?
- Is my hand pointing toward the target when I finish my throw?

CATCH AROUND

Activity Goal

To throw and catch objects while on the move.

Fundamental Movement Skills

Throwing underhand and overhand, catching

Tactical Focus

Offense: Maintain possession, create space, apply appropriate movement skills, move safely through the activity space.

Level

Exploring

Facility

Gymnasium or outdoors

Equipment

4 to 6 objects (e.g., footballs, discs, soft skin balls, basketballs)

Time

20 to 25 minutes

Activity Category

Territory

Safety

Ensure that indoor and outdoor activity spaces are a safe distance from walls and free of hazards (e.g., benches, equipment, basketball nets, holes, loose gravel, wet grass); remove or mark any hazards. Provide safe distances between groups. Remind participants to keep their heads up and to be aware of objects being thrown and others moving throughout the space.

Activity Instructions

Participants are in groups of four or five, and one person is the thrower. One at a time, group members circle the thrower, running in front to catch an underhand or overhand throw. Participants catch the object on the run and then continue running around the circle before returning the object to the thrower with another underhand or overhand throw. Change throwers after all participants have had a turn running.

Adaptations

To decrease the challenge:

- Have the catchers stand still.
- Decrease the distance between the thrower and the catchers.
- Allow the catchers to select the object (e.g., soft skin ball).

To increase the challenge:

- Increase the distance between the thrower and the catchers.
- Require one-hand catches.
- Have participants catch with their nondominant hands.

Self-Check Questions

- Do I throw the object proficiently to the catcher?
- Can I catch the object while moving?
- Do I reach out for the object when catching?
- Do my eyes follow the object until I catch it?

SPELL IT

Activity Goal

To pass an object to a teammate without the defensive team intercepting.

Fundamental Movement Skills

Throwing underhand or overhand, catching

Tactical Focus

- Offense: Create space, maintain possession.
- Defense: Regain possession, defend space.

Level

Exploring

Facility

Gymnasium or outdoors

Equipment

5 or 6 objects (e.g., soft skin balls, rubber chickens, beanbags)

Time

20 to 25 minutes

Activity Category

Territory

Safety

Ensure that indoor and outdoor activity spaces are a safe distance from walls and free of hazards (e.g., benches, equipment, basketball nets, holes, loose gravel, wet grass); remove or mark any hazards. Provide safe distances between games occurring in the same space. Remind participants to keep their heads up and to be aware of objects being thrown.

Activity Instructions

Participants form groups of six to eight and divide into two teams with one object between them. Each team has a four-letter word it must try to spell by making four successful passes without having the object intercepted by the other team. Each successful pass earns one letter, and players holding the object may not move. Require specific passes based on the learning goals (e.g., underhand, overhand, bounce pass). When a word is spelled (four passes are made), the object is dropped, or an interception is made, the other team gets possession of the object.

Adaptations

To decrease the challenge:

- Increase the size of the activity area.
- Allow players in possession of the object to take two or three steps.
- Decrease the number of passes required by having teams spell shorter words.
- Begin with three or four offensive players and one defender. Slowly increase the number of defenders.

To increase the challenge:

- Decrease the size of the activity area.
- Provide smaller objects.
- Increase the number of passes required by having teams spell longer words.
- Set a period of time in which players must pass the object.

Self-Check Questions

- Do I throw the object proficiently to my teammates?
- Do I move in a way that is safe for myself and my teammates?
- Do I reach out for the object when catching?
- Do I catch the object and hug it to my body?

NOODLE ARCHERY

Activity Goal

To accurately project a pool noodle toward a target.

Fundamental Movement Skill

Throwing overhand

Tactical Focus

Offense: Determine an appropriate distance from which to throw an object, create a dynamic reaction.

Level

Exploring

Facility

Gymnasium

Equipment

4 to 6 pool noodles, 4 to 6 hula hoops, 16 to 20 cones

Time

20 to 25 minutes

Activity Category

Target

Safety

Ensure that the activity space is a safe distance from walls and free of hazards (e.g., benches, equipment, basketball nets, poles); remove or mark any hazards. Provide safe distances between games occurring in the same space. Remind participants to keep their heads up and to be aware of noodles being thrown.

Activity Instructions

Participants form groups of four to six; then create two teams for a game. Teams place one hula hoop at the end of the activity area, with one cone in the center of the hoop. They then place three cones at various distances from the hula hoop. Team members take turns throwing the noodle overhand at the cone in the hoop from the cone of their choice to try to collect the most points. Allow teams to establish their own point systems based on the three distances of cones from the hula hoop. Noodles thrown remain on the playing area until everyone has had a turn.

Adaptations

To decrease the challenge:

- Decrease the distance between the cones and the hula hoop.
- Change the throwing object (e.g., ball, beanbag, rubber chicken).
- Adjust the scoring system.

To increase the challenge:

- Increase the distance between the cones and the hula hoop.

- Use a smaller target.
- Set a time limit and challenge players to obtain as many points as possible in that time.

Self-Check Questions
- Do I throw the noodle proficiently toward the target?
- Do I apply the required amount of force to get the noodle to the target?
- Do I know my strength and throw from the cone I will be most successful from?
- Do I follow through toward the target when I release the noodle?

BASKETBALL GOLF

Activity Goal
To accurately throw a basketball toward a target.

Fundamental Movement Skill
Throwing underhand and overhand

Tactical Focus
Offense: Determine an appropriate distance from which to throw an object, avoid obstacles.

Level
Competent

Facility
Gymnasium

Equipment
20 or 30 basketballs (1 per participant), 4 to 6 basketball nets, 9 cones

Time
30 to 35 minutes

Activity Category
Target

Safety

Ensure that the indoor activity space is a safe distance from hazards (e.g., walls, equipment, benches); remove or mark any hazards. Provide safe distances between holes. Remind participants to keep their heads up and to be aware of basketballs being shot.

Activity Instructions

Use cones to mark nine places on the court to serve as holes, and number them from 1 to 9. Multiple holes can be set up at the same basket. Working in pairs or small groups, participants shoot from each hole until they make a basket. They may catch their own rebounds and take the next shot from that spot. Once the basket is made, the partner or another group member shoots from the hole; when both (or all) players have made a basket, the pair or group determines how many shots they took cumulatively. Consider having pairs or groups record their total shots on a basketball golf tee card. Once pairs or groups have completed a hole, they move to the next one. Allow pairs or groups to move through the holes in any order to avoid backups and increase active participation.

> *Basketball learning cues: Keep the feet shoulder-width apart, bend the knees, position the elbow under the ball, push the ball upward with the shooting hand, release the ball, follow through toward the target.*

Adaptations

To decrease the challenge:

- Decrease the distances between the holes and the net.
- Hang a hula hoop on the net as the target.
- Have participants play best ball by using the lowest score per hole.

To increase the challenge:

- Increase the distances between the holes and the net.
- Keep individual scores instead of team scores.
- Require players to use their nondominant hands.

Self-Check Questions

- Do I shoot the ball toward the target proficiently?
- Do I apply the required amount of force to send the ball to the target?
- Do I follow through toward the target?

Activity Goal

To complete as many passes as possible.

Fundamental Movement Skills

Throwing overhand and underhand, catching

Tactical Focus

Offense: Perform appropriate movement skills, move safely throughout the space.

Level

Proficient

Facility

Gymnasium or outdoors

Equipment

15 to 18 balls (various sizes), baseball gloves (optional)

Time

5 to 20 minutes

Activity Category

Striking/fielding

Safety

Ensure that indoor and outdoor activity spaces are a safe distance from walls and free of hazards (e.g., benches, equipment, basketball nets, holes, loose gravel, wet grass); remove or mark any hazards. Provide safe distances between groups. Remind participants to keep their heads up and to be aware of balls being thrown.

Activity Instructions

Groups with odd numbers (five or seven) form circles. The designated first thrower in each group has all three balls and tosses one to a team-mate on the opposite side of the circle. That person catches and throws the ball to a different person as a throwing pattern begins to form.

Players must remember who threw to them and to whom they threw throughout the drill, because this pattern will be used throughout the activity. Players may not throw to teammates on either side of them. Remind participants to wait until the receiving person is looking at them before throwing. After some practice, consider adding the second and then the third ball. Challenge groups to complete as many successful passes as possible within a given period of time. If the ball is dropped the group will start counting again from zero.

Adaptations

To decrease the challenge:

- Decrease the size of the circles.
- Have players use an underhand throw.
- Use larger or softer balls.

To increase the challenge:

- Increase the size of the circles.
- Require that players use only one hand to throw or catch.
- Have players use an overhand throw.

Self-Check Questions

- Am I able to apply controlled force to send the ball to my teammates?
- Am I in an active stance ready to catch the ball?
- Do I communicate well with teammates both verbally and nonverbally?

THROW VOLLEYBALL

Activity Goal

To throw an object into the defensive team's court in such a way that it cannot be returned.

Fundamental Movement Skills

Throwing underhand and overhand, catching

Tactical Focus

- Offense: Set up for an attack.
- Defense: Defend against an attack.

Level

Competent

Facility

Gymnasium or outdoors

Equipment

5 or 6 balls (various sizes), volleyball nets, volleyball poles, safety mats to wrap around poles

Time

30 to 35 minutes

Activity Category

Net/wall

Safety

Ensure that indoor and outdoor activity spaces are a safe distance from walls and free of hazards (e.g., benches, equipment, basketball nets, holes, loose gravel, wet grass); remove or mark any hazards. Provide safe distances between games occurring in the same space. Remind participants to keep their heads up and to be aware of objects being thrown.

Activity Instructions

Working in teams of four to six, two teams throw the ball over the net so that it strikes the floor or ground on the opposite side. The game begins with one team throwing (i.e., serving) the ball over the net and the defenders try to catch it before it hits the floor or ground. Three players per side must catch and throw the ball before they can send it back over the net, and each player may touch the ball only once per rally. Points are awarded on the serve when the defenders let the ball touch the floor or ground. Games continue until 25 is scored, or for an appropriate amount of time.

Adaptations

To decrease the challenge:

- Use an alternative object (e.g., beach ball, balloon).
- Allow participants to determine the scoring.
- Allow one bounce per rally.

To increase the challenge:

- Decrease the size of the activity area.
- Use a volleyball.
- Have participants volley the ball instead of throwing and catching

Self-Check Questions

- Do I throw the ball proficiently over the net?
- Do I throw the ball so that opponents are unable to catch the ball?
- Am I in an active stance ready to catch the ball?
- Do I communicate well with teammates both verbally and nonverbally?

ULTIMATE FOOTBALL

Activity Goal

To invade the opponent's end zone to score.

Fundamental Movement Skills

Kicking, throwing, catching

Tactical Focus

- Offense: Create space, attack the goal.
- Defense: Set plays, defend space.

Level

Competent

Facility

Outdoors

Equipment

4 to 6 footballs, 16 to 24 cones, 12 to 18 pinnies

Time

30 to 35 minutes

Activity Category

Territory

Safety

Ensure that activity spaces are a safe distance from walls and free of hazards (e.g., benches, equipment, holes, loose gravel, wet grass); remove or mark any hazards. Provide safe distances between games occurring in the same space. Remind participants to keep their heads up and to be aware of footballs being thrown and players moving throughout the activity space.

Activity Instructions

Use cones to mark multiple rectangular playing areas that have two opposing end zones. Two teams of four to six have one ball and play in each area. The game begins with the first team kicking off to the second. Players on the second team receive the ball and take three steps before they must throw the ball to a teammate. Teams attempt to pass the ball into the opposing team's end zone, where it is caught by a teammate. Opponents work to intercept the ball in the air; they may not touch players who are throwing. If a ball is dropped or intercepted, the opposing team receives possession at the point of drop or interception. Following a point, teams change direction as the scoring team kicks off to the opposing team. Games continue until 15 points are scored, or for an appropriate amount of time. Consider using pinnies to distinguish teams.

Adaptations

To decrease the challenge:

- Decrease the size of the playing area.
- Choose an alternative throwing object (e.g., beach ball, beanbag, soft skin ball).
- Vary the type of throw (e.g., underhand, chest pass).

To increase the challenge:

- Set a period of time in which participants must pass the ball.
- Identify a number of passes that must be made before a team can score.
- Require players to use their nondominant hands.

Self-Check Questions

- Can I make short, quick passes to move the ball into the opposing team's territory?
- Am I in an active stance ready to catch the ball?
- Do I create offensive space by placing the ball away from defenders?
- Am I able to communicate with teammates to maintain possession of the ball?

END BALL

Activity Goal

To invade the opponent's end zone to score.

Fundamental Movement Skills

Throwing underhand and overhand, catching

Tactical Focus

- Offense: Create space, attack the goal, set plays.
- Defense: Set plays.

Level

Proficient

Facility

Gymnasium or outdoors

Equipment

5 to 7 balls (various sizes), 20 to 30 cones

Time

20 to 25 minutes

Activity Category

Territory

Safety

Ensure that indoor and outdoor activity spaces are a safe distance from walls and free of hazards (e.g., benches, equipment, basketball nets, holes, loose gravel, wet grass); remove or mark any hazards. Provide safe distances between games occurring in the same space. Remind participants to keep their heads up and to be aware of balls being thrown.

Activity Instructions

Use cones to mark square playing areas with two opposing end zones. Two teams of four to six with one ball play in each area. Teams attempt to pass the ball into the opposing team's end zone, where it is caught by a teammate who touches it to the ground to score. Opponents work to intercept the ball in the air; they may not touch players who are throwing. Require that players use a specific pass based on learning goals (e.g., underhand, overhand, short rugby pass, bounce pass). Players in possession of the ball cannot move. If a ball is dropped or intercepted, the opposing team receives possession at the point of the drop or interception. The opposing team gets possession of the ball following a score. Games continue until 15 is scored, or for an appropriate amount of time.

Adaptations

To decrease the challenge:

- Decrease the distance between the end zones.
- Have teams use more than one ball.
- Add a second end zone for each team.

To increase the challenge:

- Increase the distance between the end zones.
- Impose a time limit in which teams must score.
- Require that players use their nondominant hands.

Self-Check Questions

- Am I able to apply controlled force to send the ball to my teammates?
- Do I move to an open space to receive the ball?
- Can I transition quickly from offense to defense?

BEANBAG CURLING

Activity Goal

To send an object to a target and to accumulate the most points.

Fundamental Movement Skill

Throwing underhand

Tactical Focus

Offense: Perform appropriate movement skills, move safely throughout the space, get the last shot to create a dynamic reaction, avoid obstacles

Level

Proficient

Facility

Gymnasium or outdoors

Equipment

16 beanbags, 2 cones, and 2 hoops (per game of 8 players), skipping ropes or floor tape

Time

20 to 25 minutes

Activity Category

Target

Safety

Ensure that indoor and outdoor activity spaces are a safe distance from walls and free of hazards (e.g., benches, equipment, basketball nets, holes, loose gravel, wet grass); remove or mark any hazards. Provide safe distances between games occurring in the same space. Remind participants to keep their heads up and to be aware of beanbags being slid.

Activity Instructions

Divide participants into groups of eight. Then divide each group into two teams of four, and give each team eight beanbags. Each team creates a house with three concentric layers using tape, hula hoops, or skipping ropes, and places a cone in the center. Teams alternate turns throwing a beanbag to get it as close to the cone (the center of the house) as possible. Teams score points for each beanbag that is closer to the center than the closest beanbag of the opposing team. Only beanbags inside the house score points.

Adaptations

To decrease the challenge:
- Decrease the distance between the throwers and the houses.
- Allow underhand throws.
- Use a larger target.

To increase the challenge:
- Increase the distance between the throwers and the houses.
- Require that players use their nondominant hands.
- Decrease the size of the houses.

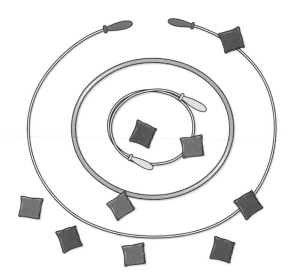

Self-Check Questions

- Am I able to apply controlled force to send the beanbag to the target?
- Do I apply tactics to increase my chances of hitting a target when other beanbags are in the way?
- Do I communicate well with teammates both verbally and nonverbally?
- Do I place beanbags strategically to make it challenging for my opponents to get close to the house?

AROUND THE BASES

Activity Goal

To score as many runs as possible.

Fundamental Movement Skills

Throwing underhand or overhand, catching

Tactical Focus

- Offense: Score runs, avoid getting out.
- Defense: Stop runs from scoring.

Level

Proficient

Facility

Outdoors

Equipment

5 to 7 balls (various sizes), 20 to 30 bases or cones

Time

20 to 25 minutes

Activity Category

Striking/fielding

Safety

Ensure that activity spaces are a safe distance from walls and free of hazards (e.g., benches, equipment, holes, loose gravel, wet grass); remove or mark any hazards. Provide safe distances between games occurring in the same space. Remind participants to keep their heads up and to be aware of balls being thrown and teammates moving throughout the activity space.

Activity Instructions

Working in groups of five, participants set up three bases and a home base in their activity spaces. The setup is similar to baseball, but the distance between the bases is reduced to accommodate multiple playing areas.

Four players occupy the three bases and home base as throwers; the fifth player is the runner starting from home base. The runner shouts "Go" and proceeds to run the bases (as in a home run) while the throwers attempt to throw the ball around the bases twice before the runner reaches home. If the runner (running once around the bases) beats the ball (being thrown twice around the bases), players change positions. Consider setting up safety zones near the bases to keep the runner a safe distance from the balls being thrown in order to avoid being struck by the ball.

Adaptations

To decrease the challenge:

- Decrease the distance between the bases.

- Have players use an underhand throw.
- Require throwers to throw the ball three times around the bases before the runner runs once around the bases.

To increase the challenge:

- Increase the distance between the bases.
- Change the ball to a smaller object (e.g., Wiffle ball, beanbag, tennis ball).
- Add a second ball.

Self-Check Questions

- Do I apply controlled force to send the ball to my teammates?
- Do I move to an open space to receive the ball?
- Can I run quickly to score runs?

KNOCK OUT

Activity Goal

To pass the object into the opponents' end zone.

Fundamental Movement Skills

Throwing underhand and overhand, catching

Tactical Focus

- Offense: Create space, attack the goal.
- Defense: Set plays.

Level

Proficient

Facility

Gymnasium or outdoors

Equipment

1 object per game (e.g., soccer ball, football, disc), 12 to 16 cones

Time

15 to 20 minutes

Activity Category

Territory

Safety

Ensure that indoor and outdoor activity spaces are a safe distance from walls and free of hazards (e.g., benches, equipment, basketball nets, holes, loose gravel, wet grass); remove or mark any hazards. Provide safe distances between games occurring in the same space. Remind participants to keep their heads up and to be aware of objects being thrown and players moving throughout the activity space.

Activity Instructions

Two teams of six to eight participants play across the width of the gym or field, with a cone-marked neutral zone in the center. Three or four players from each team stand on each end of the space. Players try to pass the ball over the neutral zone to teammates, while defenders attempt to knock it out of the air. When a ball is knocked out, the first team to touch it gets possession. Teams score 1 point for every successful pass. If a ball thrown across the neutral zone is caught by the opposing team, that team earns 2 points.

Adaptations

To decrease the challenge:

- Add a second ball.
- Decrease the size of the neutral zone.

To increase the challenge:

- Increase the size of the neutral zone.
- Have players send the ball a different way (e.g., using the non-dominant hand or an overhand throw).

Self-Check Questions

- Am I able to place the ball away from defenders? (offense)
- Am I using the full playing area to create space? (offense)
- Am I rebounding dropped balls to get or maintain possession? (offense)
- Am I covering space and my opponents? (defense)

CHAPTER 7

Striking With Hands

This chapter emphasizes the fundamental movement skill of striking an object with the hand(s), including the overhead volley in volleyball and the dribble in basketball. Participants use eye–hand coordination while tracking an incoming object and sending an object to a specific area or target. While exploring these two sending skills, participants apply the movement concept of effort awareness (e.g., time and force).

In the activities in this chapter, participants send objects such as a volleyballs and basketballs over a net to a teammate or to a target. Less experienced participants can develop striking skills by using lightweight objects such as beach balls and balloons. In most activities, individual participants set their own challenge levels by choosing among ball types, sizes, and colors, as well as the size and proximity of their targets.

Words to Know

- **Carrying.** A game violation in which players continue to dribble after the ball has come to rest in one or both hands.
- **Control dribble.** A dribble, used when a player is stationary or closely guarded, in which the ball is kept low and close to the body.
- **Double dribbling.** An illegal dribble that occurs when a player dribbles with both hands or stops and then resumes dribbling.
- **Dribbling with hands.** Moving an object forward with continuous slight touches of the hand.
- **Overhead volley.** The motion of striking an object with the hands while it is in the air.
- **Power dribble.** An intense dribble, used when moving quickly, in which the ball rebounds to hip height and is pushed in front of the body.

Overhead Volley Transferable Skills

Preparation	Execution	Follow-Through
1. Adopt an athletic stance (e.g., strong base of support, feet shoulder-width apart, knees slightly bent). 2. Square shoulders and feet to the target. 3. Extend the hands 6 inches (15 cm) above the forehead. 4. Keep the eyes on the target.	1. Push the fingers up and outward at ball contact. 2. Apply force to send the ball in the direction of the target.	1. Extend arms with thumbs and palms facing the target. 2. Readopt an athletic stance (e.g., strong base of support, balanced) to be in position to perform the next movement.

Overhead volley learning cues: Face the target, keep the eyes on the ball, get underneath the ball, extend the hands above the head, extend the legs, push the fingers up and out toward the target.

Dribbling With Hands Transferable Skills

Preparation	Execution	Follow-Through
1. Maintain a low athletic stance (e.g., strong base of support, balanced). 2. Keep the head up and look around. 3. Contact the ball with the fingertips, pushing it down and slightly forward with a controlled motion of the wrist and forearm.	Keep the ball under control (i.e., close to the body) using the fingertips. Keep the fingers spread and relaxed.	1. Absorb the bounce with the arm, wrist, and fingers. 2. Keep the ball below the waist.

Dribbling with hands learning cues: Contact the ball with the fingertips, keep the head up, push the ball down and slightly forward, keep the ball below the waist.

Where's The Physical Literacy?

Striking with the hand(s) is a fundamental movement skill commonly used in games to send objects to teammates, opponents, or targets. This advanced skill requires a combination of eye–hand coordination and the ability to track an incoming ball and send it in one motion. While striking, participants explore the movement concept of effort awareness as they play with time (e.g., slow, medium, fast) and force (e.g., light, strong). They also explore movement principles such as the law of reaction/force (i.e., an object usually moves in the direction opposite that of the applied force), impulse-causing momentum (i.e., the greater the applied impulse, the greater the increase in motion), center of gravity (i.e., when struck in line with its center of gravity, an object will travel in a straight line), and inertia (i.e., continued force is needed to keep an object moving).

Educator Check and Reflect

Overhead Volley

- When appropriate, use smaller badminton nets.
- Give participants a choice of objects as often as possible (e.g., soft touch volleyball, beach ball, balloon).
- Help participants develop critical thinking skills by focusing on game strategies throughout the activity.
- Make sure that balls not in play are retrieved from the activity area immediately to avoid injuries.
- Always emphasize safety and ball control.

Dribble

- Consider using a variety of basketball sizes. Smaller balls are easier to control.
- Emphasize the need to look ahead when dribbling.
- Encourage competent participants to use fakes prior to passing the ball, before and during dribbling, and before and during shooting.
- Encourage the use of an athletic stance when receiving a pass.
- Help participants develop critical thinking skills by focusing on game strategies throughout the activity.
- Encourage participants to watch a basketball game (online or on TV) with a focus on how players dribble, pass, and communicate with teammates.
- Always emphasize safety and ball control.

VOLLEY WITH LOVE

Activity Goal

To see how many times a balloon can be hit before touching the floor.

Fundamental Movement Skill

Overhead volleying

Tactical Focus

Offense: Maintain consistency when overhead volleying.

Level

Beginning

Facility

Gymnasium

Equipment

6 to 8 balloons, 6 cones per group

Time

15 to 20 minutes

Activity Category

Net/wall

Safety

Ensure that the indoor activity space is a safe distance from walls and free of hazards (e.g., benches, equipment, basketball nets); remove or mark any hazards. Provide safe distances between groups in the same space. Remind participants to keep their heads up and to be aware of others when moving through the space.

Activity Instructions

Participants create groups of four, and form pairs. Each group creates a small court using cones to mark the external boundaries and two cones through the center to act as the net. Each group has one balloon. The first pair volleys a balloon into the opponent's court. The retrieving pair must hit the balloon three times before returning it to the other court.

Groups work together to maintain a rally and count the number of consecutive hits they make together.

Adaptations

To decrease the challenge:

- Decrease the size of the court.
- Remove the cones acting as nets and focus participants on keeping the balloon afloat.
- Have participants throw with both hands or roll the balloon.

To increase the challenge:

- Increase the size of the court.
- Use a net or bench to divide the playing area.
- Use a soft ball instead of a balloon.

Self-Check Questions

- Do I apply the amount of force needed for the balloon to reach my opponent?
- Do I change my position based on the location of the balloon?
- Do I get under the balloon before returning it to my opponents?

DRIBBLE TAG

Activity Goal

To maintain control of the ball while playing tag.

Fundamental Movement Skill

Dribbling

Tactical Focus

Offense: Maintain possession.

Level

Beginning

Facility

Gymnasium

Equipment

20 to 30 basketballs (various sizes)

Time

15 to 20 minutes

Activity Category

Territory

Safety

Ensure that the space is a safe distance from hazards (e.g., walls, equipment, debris); remove or mark any hazards. Remind participants to keep their heads up and be aware of balls and other participants moving throughout the activity space.

Activity Instructions

Designate four or five participants to be taggers, and give everyone else a basketball. Participants dribble around the gymnasium keeping control of their balls. Tagged participants must perform four passes with their taggers before changing roles with them.

Adaptations

To decrease the challenge:

- Decrease the size of the activity space.
- Provide larger balls.
- Provide equipment so participants can dribble in different ways (e.g., with feet in soccer, with a stick in hockey).

To increase the challenge:

- Increase the size of the activity space.
- Increase the number of taggers.
- Have participants dribble with their nondominant hands.

Self-Check Questions

- Do I keep my head up while dribbling?
- Do I use one hand to protect the ball?
- Do I make quick decisions while moving with the ball?

FREEZE COUNT

Activity Goal

To maintain control of the ball while dribbling around a partner.

Fundamental Movement Skill

Dribbling

Tactical Focus

Offense: Maintain possession.

Level

Beginning

Facility

Gymnasium or outdoors

Equipment

15 to 20 basketballs (various sizes)

Time

15 to 20 minutes

Activity Category

Territory

Safety

Ensure that indoor and outdoor activity spaces are a safe distance from walls and free of hazards (e.g., benches, equipment, basketball nets, holes, loose gravel); remove or mark any hazards. Provide safe distances between pairs. Remind participants to keep their heads up and to be aware of others when moving through the space.

Activity Instructions

Participants work in pairs facing each other. Partner A dribbles around partner B, who counts out loud the number of seconds it takes to return to the original position. Then partners switch roles. Partner B might perform a physical task (e.g., jumping jack, squat) while counting. Participants try to improve their time each round. Remind participants to move at a speed that allows them to maintain control of the ball while also moving quickly.

Adaptations

To decrease the challenge:

- Decrease the distance between partners.
- Use a different type of ball.
- Provide equipment so participants can dribble in different ways (e.g., with feet in soccer, with a stick in hockey).

To increase the challenge:

- Increase the distance between partners.
- Require participants to dribble with their nondominant hands.
- Add a third participant, who attempts to intercept the ball.

Self-Check Questions

- Do I keep my head up while dribbling?
- Do I use one hand to protect the ball?
- Do I make quick decisions while moving with the ball?

PASS THROUGH

Activity Goal

To score goals by invading the opponent's area.

Fundamental Movement Skill

Dribbling

Tactical Focus

- Offense: Attack the goal.
- Defense: Defend space.

Level

Exploring

Facility

Gymnasium or outdoors

Equipment

6 to 8 basketballs (various sizes)

Time

15 to 20 minutes

Activity Category

Territory

Safety

Ensure that indoor and outdoor activity spaces are a safe distance from walls and free of hazards (e.g., benches, equipment, basketball nets, holes, loose gravel); remove or mark any hazards. Provide safe distances between games in the same space. Remind participants to keep their heads up and be aware of balls and other participants moving throughout the activity space.

Activity Instructions

Divide participants into teams of three. Teams pair up and form a circle, facing each other; each team has a basketball. Each team dribbles and passes the ball amongst teammates before attempting to send it between the opponents on the other half of the circle. Opponents try to defend their space; however, once a ball passes through the opponents' side, the opponents gain possession. Teams can be in possession of two balls at once. Teams earn 1 point for each pass-through.

Adaptations

To decrease the challenge:

- Decrease the size of the circle.
- Have players roll the balls.
- Change the type of ball.

To increase the challenge:

- Increase the size of the circle.
- Keep individual scores instead of team scores.
- Have players use more than one ball.

Self-Check Questions

- Do I keep my head up while dribbling?
- Do I make quick decisions while moving with the ball?
- Do I use the required amount of force to send the ball into the designated space?
- Do I follow through toward the designated space when I release the ball?

MULTIBALL BEACH BALL VOLLEYBALL

Activity Goal

To score by landing a ball in the opponents' court.

Fundamental Movement Skill

Overhead volleying

Tactical Focus

- Offense: Maintain consistency when overhead volleying, set up for an attack.
- Defense: Defend space, defend against an attack.

Level

Exploring

Facility

Gymnasium or outdoors

Equipment

6 to 9 balls of various kinds (e.g., beach balls, volleyballs, soft skin balls), volleyball nets, poles covered with mats

Time

20 to 25 minutes

Activity Category

Territory

Safety

Ensure that indoor and outdoor activity spaces are a safe distance from walls and free of hazards (e.g., benches, equipment, basketball nets, holes, loose gravel, wet grass); remove or mark any hazards. Provide safe distances between games in the same space. Remind participants to keep their heads up and be aware of balls being volleyed.

Activity Instructions

Groups of four to six scatter on each side of a court with one ball per game. The game begins with a player in the front right position serving the ball by throwing it over the net into the opposite court. Opposing players try to volley the ball back over the net without letting it touch the floor or ground. Each player may hit the ball only once per rally, but any number of players may hit it before it goes over the net. After a few rallies, add a second and then a third ball.

As appropriate, consider introducing scoring:

- Games are played to 25 points.
- Points are awarded on the serve when the other team lets the ball touch the floor or ground.

Adaptations

To decrease the challenge:

- Use a different object (e.g., beach ball or balloon).
- Allow participants to determine scoring.
- Allow one bounce per rally.

To increase the challenge:

- Decrease the size of the activity area.
- Use a volleyball.
- Require a designated number of hits per side.

Self-Check Questions
- Can I volley the ball over the net?
- Do I make a triangle shape with my thumbs and index fingers?
- Do I move so that I am underneath the ball when I volley?
- Do I follow through at the moment of impact to send the ball up and over the net?

VOLLEY UP AND RUN

Activity Goal
To send the ball to the leader using a volley.

Fundamental Movement Skill
Overhead volleying

Tactical Focus
Offense: Maintain consistency when overhead volleying.

Level
Exploring

Facility
Gymnasium or outdoors

Equipment
5 or 6 balls (e.g., volleyballs, soft skin balls, beach balls)

Time
15 to 20 minutes

Activity Category
Territory

Safety
Ensure that indoor and outdoor activity spaces are a safe distance from walls and free of hazards (e.g., benches, equipment, basketball nets,

holes, loose gravel, wet grass); remove or mark any hazards. Provide safe distances between groups in the same space. Remind participants to keep their heads up and be aware of balls being volleyed and other participants moving throughout the activity space.

Activity Instructions

Create groups of four or five players who stand behind each other in a line. Each team selects a leader who stands facing the other group mates about 10 feet (3 m) away. The leader tosses the ball to the first participant, who volleys it back to the leader and quickly runs to the end of the line. When the first participant returns to the front of the line, that person becomes the leader.

Adaptations

To decrease the challenge:

- Let participants choose an object to receive (e.g., balloon, beach ball).
- Allow one bounce before receiving the ball.
- Permit players to catch the ball before throwing it back to the leader.

To increase the challenge:

- Keep score of consecutive volleys.
- Increase the distance between the leader and the rest of the group.
- Introduce an implement for sending the ball back to the leader (e.g., table tennis paddle, tennis racket, badminton racket).

Self-Check Questions

- Do I move so that I am underneath the ball when I volley?
- Do I make a triangle shape with my thumbs and index fingers?
- Do I follow through at the moment of impact to send the ball upward to the leader?

Activity Goal

To maintain possession of the ball as long as possible. To score on the opposing team.

Fundamental Movement Skill

Dribbling

Tactical Focus

- Offense: Maintain possession.
- Defense: Regain possession.

Level

Competent

Facility

Gymnasium or outdoors

Equipment

4 to 6 basketballs (various sizes, 1 per game), 2 dice per game, basketball nets

Time

15 to 20 minutes

Activity Category

Territory

Safety

Ensure that indoor and outdoor activity spaces are a safe distance from walls and free of hazards (e.g., benches, equipment, basketball nets, holes, loose gravel); remove or mark any hazards. Provide safe distances between games occurring in the same space. Remind participants to keep their heads up and to be aware of balls and other participants when moving through the space.

Activity Instructions

Participants form teams of six to eight and pair up with other teams for games of modified basketball. Each team rolls a die to reveal the number of players who will participate in the game (possibly creating uneven teams). Players dribble and pass the ball to teammates to maintain possession, and both teams score on the same net. After one minute of play, the two dice are rolled to identify the number of participants for the next game.

Adaptations

To decrease the challenge:

- Decrease the size of the playing area.
- Have the same number of participants on each team.
- Change the type of ball (e.g., soft skin ball).

To increase the challenge:

- Increase the size of the playing area.
- Use different games to modify the method of dribbling (e.g., hockey, soccer).
- Have players dribble with their nondominant hands.

Self-Check Questions

- Do I move to an open space to receive the ball?
- Do I communicate to my teammates when I am open to receive a pass?
- Do I make quick decisions about moving and passing?
- Do I use passing and faking strategies to find open space?

TRIANGLES

Activity Goal

To send the ball accurately to a target.

Fundamental Movement Skill

Overhead volleying

Tactical Focus

- Offense: Maintain consistency when overhead volleying, set up an attack.
- Defense: Defend against an attack.

Level
Competent

Facility
Gymnasium or outdoors

Equipment
8 to 10 volleyballs (1 per participant)

Activity Category
Net/wall

Safety
Ensure that indoor and outdoor activity spaces are a safe distance from walls and free of hazards (e.g., benches, equipment, basketball nets, holes, loose gravel, wet grass); remove or mark any hazards. Provide safe distances between groups in the same space. Remind participants to keep their heads up and be aware of volleyballs being volleyed.

Time
15 to 20 minutes

Activity Instructions
Working in groups of three, participants toss a ball to each other, attempting to catch it at their forehead with hands in proper triangle formation in preparation for the overhead volley. Participants toss the ball back from its position at their foreheads. The focus is on bending the knees and then using the shoulders, elbows, wrists, and fingers. Participants gradually increase the speed of the toss and catch, increase the distance of the toss, and change the direction of the toss (e.g., from side to side). Encourage participants to focus on aim and accuracy.

Next, two participants take turns volleying back and forth while the third participant is between them trying to block the volley. If the volley is blocked, the blocker changes positions with the participant whose ball was blocked. Change roles often.

Adaptations
To decrease the challenge:
- Substitute a lighter object to hit (e.g., balloon, beach ball).
- Allow one bounce between hits.

To increase the challenge:

- Add cones or a net between partners.
- Keep track of the number of consecutive volleys.
- Add a physical challenge (e.g., touch the floor, turn around once) before or after the volley.

Self-Check Questions

- Do I volley the ball proficiently toward my partner?
- Do I make a triangle shape with my thumbs and index fingers?
- Do I keep my eyes on the ball?
- Do I follow through at the moment of impact to send the ball up toward my partner?

UMBRELLA DRILL

Activity Goal

To send the ball to the leader using a volley.

Fundamental Movement Skill

Overhead volleying

Tactical Focus

- Offense: Maintain consistency when overhead volleying.
- Defense: Defend against an attack.

Level

Competent

Facility

Gymnasium or outdoors

Equipment

5 to 7 volleyballs

Time

15 to 20 minutes

Activity Category

Net/wall

Safety

Ensure that indoor and outdoor activity spaces are a safe distance from walls and free of hazards (e.g., benches, equipment, basketball nets, holes, loose gravel, wet grass); remove or mark any hazards. Provide safe distances between groups in the same space. Remind participants to keep their heads up and be aware of volleyballs being hit throughout the activity space.

Activity Instructions

Groups of five or six stand in a semicircle with one leader facing the group. The leader throws the ball to each participant, who returns it with a volley. Once all participants have had a turn, the leader and the first participant change places and the drill is repeated until all participants have had a turn as the leader. Encourage participants to focus on aim and accuracy.

Next, one participant in the semicircle tries to block the volley. If the volley is blocked, the blocker changes positions with the participant whose ball was blocked. Change roles often.

Adaptations

To decrease the challenge:

- Have participants choose the object to receive (e.g., balloon, beach ball).
- Allow one bounce before receiving the ball.
- Require that participants catch the ball before sending it to the leader.

To increase the challenge:

- Keep track of the number of consecutive volleys.
- Increase the distance between the leader and participants.
- Introduce an implement for sending the ball to the leader (e.g., table tennis paddle, tennis racket, badminton racket).

Self-Check Questions

- Do I move so that I am underneath the ball when I volley?
- Do I make a triangle shape with my thumbs and index fingers?
- Do I follow through at the moment of impact to send the ball up to the leader?

KEEP IT UP

Activity Goal

To accurately volley a ball after it bounces off a wall.

Fundamental Movement Skill

Overhead volleying

Tactical Focus

Offense: Maintain consistency when overhead volleying.

Level

Competent

Facility

Gymnasium or outdoors

Equipment

6 to 8 volleyballs

Time

15 to 20 minutes

Activity Category

Net/wall

Safety

Ensure that indoor and outdoor activity spaces are a safe distance from walls and free of hazards (e.g., benches, equipment, basketball nets, holes, loose gravel, wet grass); remove or mark any hazards. Provide safe distances between groups in the same space. Remind participants to keep their heads up and be aware of volleyballs being hit throughout the activity space.

Activity Instructions

Participants form groups of four or five and line up single file facing a wall. The first participant volleys to the wall and then runs to end of the line so the next participant can make the volley before the ball touches the ground or floor. Each time the ball drops, the team collects a letter of the phrase *Keep it up.* Participants try to collect as few letters as possible.

Adaptations

To decrease the challenge:

- Have participants choose the object to receive (e.g., balloon, beach ball).
- Allow one bounce before receiving the ball.
- Place a variety of targets on the wall.

To increase the challenge:

- Keep track of the number of consecutive volleys.
- Increase the distance from the participants to the wall.
- Introduce an implement for sending the ball to the wall (e.g., table tennis paddle, tennis racket, badminton racket).

Self-Check Questions

- Do I move so that I am underneath the ball when I volley?
- Do I make a triangle shape with my thumbs and index fingers?
- Do I follow through at the moment of impact to send the ball high on the wall?
- Do I transition quickly from volleying to my position at the end of the line?

CRAZY EIGHTS

Activity Goal

To volley as quickly and accurately as possible to get an opponent out.

Fundamental Movement Skill

Overhead volleying

Tactical Focus

Offense: Maintain consistency when volleying.

Level

Competent

Facility

Gymnasium or outdoors

Equipment

8 to 12 balls (various sizes)

Time

15 to 20 minutes

Activity Category

Net/wall

Safety

Ensure that indoor and outdoor activity spaces are a safe distance from walls and free of hazards (e.g., benches, equipment, basketball nets, holes, loose gravel, wet grass); remove or mark any hazards. Provide safe distances between groups in the same space. Remind participants to keep their heads up and be aware of balls being volleyed.

Activity Instructions

Working in groups of 8 or 10, participants form two circles (four or five participants in each) side by side with one ball per circle. Participants in each circle number off. Participants volley the ball around the circle starting with the first participant. The last person in the circle volleys the ball into the adjoining circle. Each circle attempts to volley the ball around quickly so that the opposing circle ends up with both balls.

Adaptations

To decrease the challenge:
- Reduce the distance between the teammates and teams.
- Select objects that are easier to volley (e.g., beach ball, beanbag, soft skin ball).
- Allow one bounce per rally.

To increase the challenge:
- Increase the distance between the teammates and teams.
- Add a second ball.
- Add a time limit for volleying around the circle.

Self-Check Questions

- Can I volley the ball proficiently toward my target (teammate or opposing team)?
- Do I follow through toward my teammate when I release the ball?

- Do I move in a way that is safe for myself and my teammates?
- Do I assume an athletic stance while waiting to receive the ball?

SITTING VOLLEYBALL

Activity Goal
To score by landing a ball in the opponents' court.

Fundamental Movement Skill
Overhead volleying

Tactical Focus
- Offense: Set up for an attack, win the point.
- Defense: Defend against an attack.

Level
Proficient

Facility
Gymnasium or outdoors

Equipment
4 to 6 volleyballs, 24 cones

Time
15 to 20 minutes

Activity Category
Net/wall

Safety
Ensure that indoor and outdoor activity spaces are a safe distance from walls and free of hazards (e.g., benches, equipment, basketball nets, holes, loose gravel, wet grass); remove or mark any hazards. Provide safe distances between games occurring in the same space. Remind participants to keep their heads up and be aware of volleyballs being hit throughout the activity area.

Activity Instructions

Create multiple rectangular playing areas divided in half with cones (the net). Teams of four to six sit on either side of the cones. One player volleys to serve the ball to the opponents' side of the net with the goal of making it unreturnable and thus scoring 1 point. During a rally, teams can hit the ball up to three times before sending it over the net. The rally ends when the ball touches the ground or floor, earning 1 point for the serving team. If the serve is incomplete, the other team gains possession.

Adaptations

To decrease the challenge:

- Substitute a lighter object (e.g., balloon, beach ball).
- Decrease the size of the court.
- Permit unlimited hits per side.
- Allow one bounce before a hit.

To increase the challenge:

- Use a bench or net instead of cones.
- Require a certain number of hits before sending the ball over the net.
- Add a physical challenge (e.g., doing a sit-up, spinning around once on seat) before or after a volley.

Self-Check Questions

- Do I volley the ball proficiently over the net?
- Do I adjust the force of my volley to increase the height of the ball?
- Do I assume a position of readiness to send or receive the ball?
- Do I follow through at the moment of impact to send the ball up over the net?

Activity Goal

To maintain control of the ball and score on the opposing team's net.

Fundamental Movement Skill

Dribbling

Tactical Focus

- Offense: Maintain possession, create space, attack the goal.
- Defense: Regain possession, defend the goal, set plays.

Level

Proficient

Facility

Gymnasium or outdoors

Equipment

2 to 4 basketballs (various sizes), 4 to 6 basketball nets

Time

20 to 25 minutes

Activity Category

Territory

Safety

Ensure that indoor and outdoor activity spaces are a safe distance from walls and free of hazards (e.g., benches, equipment, basketball nets, holes, loose gravel, wet grass); remove or mark any hazards. Provide safe distances between games occurring in the same space. Remind participants to keep their heads up and be aware of balls and other participants moving throughout the activity space.

Activity Instructions

Participants form teams of six to eight and pair up to play modified basketball. Half of the team members play on the court, and half play from the sidelines. Court players move up and down the court trying to score, but they may not pass directly to each other; instead, sideline players help move the ball down the court by receiving from and passing to court players. Only court players can score points. Switch court and sidelines players after every point.

Adaptations

To decrease the challenge:

- Decrease the size of the playing area.
- Use hoops hanging from nets for goals.
- Change the type of ball (e.g., soft skin ball).

To increase the challenge:

- Increase the size of the playing area.
- Permit only one type of pass (e.g., only use bounce passes).
- Limit the number of times players can pass the ball before they must attempt to score.

Self-Check Questions

- Do I move to an open space to receive the ball?
- Do I communicate to my teammates that I am open for a pass?
- Am I able to rebound the ball to maintain possession?
- Do I use passing and faking strategies to find open space?

BLOCKER

Activity Goal

To intercept the ball.

Fundamental Movement Skill

Overhead volleying

Tactical Focus

- Offense: Maintain possession.
- Defense: Regain possession.

Level

Proficient

Facility

Gymnasium or outdoors

Equipment

4 to 6 balls (e.g., volleyballs, soft skin balls, beach balls, balloons)

Time

15 to 20 minutes

Activity Category

Net/wall

Safety

Ensure that indoor and outdoor activity spaces are a safe distance from walls and free of hazards (e.g., benches, equipment, basketball nets, holes, loose gravel, wet grass); remove or mark any hazards. Provide safe distances between groups in the same space. Remind participants to keep their heads up and be aware of balls and other participants moving throughout the activity space.

Activity Instructions

Groups of five or six form a circle with one player (the blocker) in the center. The players in the circle use overhead volleys to pass a ball to each other, while the blocker tries to block the passes. Change blockers often. Consider having players keep their own personal record of the number of times they were able to block the ball while in the center.

Adaptations

To decrease the challenge:

- Decrease the size of the circle.
- Provide larger balls.
- Have players use a different way of passing (e.g., bump, underhand or overhead throw and catch).

To increase the challenge:

- Increase the size of the circle.
- Add a second blocker.
- Have blockers switch positions with players in the circle whose passes they blocked.

Self-Check Questions

- Do I move under the ball to overhead volley?
- Do I use the required amount of force to send the ball to team-mates?
- Am I able to set plays to avoid the blocker?

FOUR-PASS BASKETBALL

Activity Goal

To collect as many points as possible by maintaining possession of the ball.

Fundamental Movement Skill

Dribbling

Tactical Focus

- Offense: Maintain possession, create space, attack the goal.
- Defense: Regain possession, defend the goal, set plays.

Level

Proficient

Facility

Gymnasium or outdoors

Equipment

4 to 6 basketballs (various sizes)

Time

20 to 25 minutes

Activity Category

Territory

Safety

Ensure that indoor and outdoor activity spaces are a safe distance from walls and free of hazards (e.g., benches, equipment, basketball nets, holes, loose gravel); remove or mark any hazards. Provide safe distances between games occurring in the same space. Remind participants to keep their heads up and be aware of balls and other participants moving throughout the activity space.

Activity Instructions

Teams of three or four pair up for games. The object of the game is to maintain possession of the ball by using a dribble and pass. Players are permitted a maximum of four dribbles before they must pass to a teammate. Teams keep track of the number of completed passes before they lose possession. They receive 1 point for every successful pass and 2 points each time a receiver immediately returns a pass to the person who just passed to her.

Adaptations

To decrease the challenge:

- Decrease the size of the playing area.
- Change the type of ball (e.g., soft skin ball).

To increase the challenge:

- Increase the size of the playing area.
- Allow only one kind of pass (e.g., only chest passes).
- Increase the number of defensive players.
- Create goals by placing several cones about 3 feet (1 m) apart as gates around the outside of the playing areas. Have dribblers see how many gates they can get through in a set amount of time.

Self-Check Questions

- Do I make quick decisions about moving and passing?
- Do I use the required amount of force to send the ball to my teammates?
- Do I use passing and faking strategies to find open space?

CHAPTER 8

Striking With an Implement or Feet

This chapter addresses the fundamental movement skills of striking an object with an implement and with the feet. In games such as ringette and hockey, participants explore partner and small-group games in which they use implements to strike, dribble, and trap objects. In games involving striking with the feet (e.g., soccer), participants explore kicking, foot dribbling, and trapping objects. While exploring these two sending skills, participants apply the movement concept of effort awareness (e.g., time and force) while also developing eye–hand and eye–foot coordination.

In most activities, individual participants set their own challenge levels by choosing their own implements or objects (e.g., ball or ring types, sizes, and colors), as well as the size and proximity of their targets.

Words to Know

- **Dribbling with feet.** Moving an object forward with continuous slight touches of the feet.
- **Kicking.** Striking an object with the foot to propel it forward.
- **Striking with an implement.** Using an implement to hit an object to move it toward a desired object, person, or area.
- **Trapping.** Stopping the momentum of an object with the foot.
- **Trapping with an implement.** Stopping the momentum of an object with an implement.

Striking Transferable Skills

Preparation	Execution	Follow-Through
1. Adopt an athletic stance (e.g., strong base of support, balanced). 2. Stand sideways to the object. 3. Place the dominant hand at the top of the stick and the nondominant hand farther down the stick. 4. Lift the object up and back using trunk rotation. 5. Keep the eyes on the target.	1. Use the hips, trunk, shoulders, elbow, and wrists to create power during the swing and shot. 2. Move the body weight forward to produce force in the direction of the target.	1. Follow through in the direction of the target. 2. Readopt the athletic stance (e.g., strong base of support, balanced) with the object in position to perform the next movement.

Striking with an implement learning cues: Grip with the dominant hand on top, keep the eyes on the object, shift the body weight from back to front, follow through in the direction of the target.

Trapping With an Implement
Transferable Skills

1. Move the body in the path of the object.
2. Adopt an athletic stance (e.g., strong base of support, balanced).
3. Present a flat stick surface for the trap or block.
4. Keep the eyes on the object until contact is made.
5. Absorb the momentum of the object with the entire body on contact.

Trapping with an implement learning cues: Move the body in the path of the object, maintain a wide base of support, present a large surface for the trap or block, keep the eyes on the object, absorb the momentum with the body on contact.

Kicking Transferable Skills

Preparation	Execution	Follow-Through
1. Adopt an athletic stance (e.g., strong base of support, balanced). 2. Place the nonkicking foot to the side of the ball. 3. Keep the eyes on the ball. 4. Bend at the hip and knee during the backswing.	1. Ensure that the force comes from the hip and knee action. 2. Contact a low ball with the shoelace area, a high ball with the toe, and a ground ball with the inside of the foot.	1. Follow through in the direction of the target. 2. Readopt an athletic stance (e.g., strong base of support, balanced) with the ball in position to perform the next movement.

Kicking learning cues: Keep the eyes on the ball, step forward placing the nonkicking foot next to the ball, swing the kicking leg back and bring it forward fast to contact the ball, follow through in the direction of the target.

Dribbling With Feet Transferable Skills

Preparation	Execution
1. Adopt an athletic stance (e.g., strong base of support, balanced).	1. Keep the ball under control (i.e., close to the body).
2. Push the ball forward.	2. Protect the ball with the body (i.e., keep the body between the ball and the defender).
3. Keep the head up while pushing the ball.	

Dribbling with feet learning cues: Keep the ball close to the body, touch the sides of the ball using both feet.

Trapping With Feet Transferable Skills

Foot Trapping	Chest Trapping	Inside of Thigh Trapping
1. Move the body in the path of the ball.	1. Move the body in the path of the ball.	1. Move the body in the path of the ball.
2. Present the foot to trap the ball.	2. Present the chest to trap the ball.	2. Present the inside of the thigh to trap the ball.
3. Keep the eyes on the ball until contact is made.	3. Keep the eyes on the ball until contact is made.	3. Keep the eyes on the ball until contact is made.
4. On contact, draw the foot back to absorb the ball.	4. Meet the ball with the chest squared to the ball.	4. Bring the ball down with the inside of the thigh or calf.
5. Keep the heel down to keep the ball from passing underfoot.	5. Relax the chest on contact to cushion the ball.	5. Relax the thigh on contact to cushion the ball.
6. Relax the foot on contact to cushion the ball.		

Trapping with feet learning cues: Move the body in the path of the ball, present a large surface area to trap the ball (e.g., side of the foot, thigh, trunk), deflect the ball downward, keep the eyes on the ball, cushion the ball with the body.

Where's the Physical Literacy?

Striking with a foot or an implement is a fundamental movement skill commonly used in games to send an object to a teammate, opponent, or target. It requires a combination of eye–hand or eye–foot coordination and the ability to track an incoming object and send that object away.

While striking with the feet or an implement, participants explore the movement concept of effort awareness as they play with time (e.g., slow, medium, fast) and force (e.g., light, strong). They also explore movement principles such as the law of reaction/force (i.e., an object usually moves in the direction opposite that of the applied force), impulse-causing momentum (i.e., the greater the applied impulse, the greater the increase in motion), center of gravity (i.e., when struck in line with its center of gravity, an object will travel in a straight line), and inertia (i.e., continued force is needed to keep an object moving).

Educator Check and Reflect: Striking With an Implement

- Follow administration policy regarding equipment. Consider using only commercially produced floor hockey or hockey stick shafts with protective coverings on the ends (e.g., a piece of sponge or carpet taped on) and ringette sticks.
- Check sticks regularly for splinters and cracks.
- Require that sticks be in contact with the floor at all times while participants are on the move. During shots or passes, sticks may not go above waist level.
- Allow no contact between sticks and bodies. Establish rules for stick infractions, and enforce them.
- Always emphasize safety and object control.
- When using goalies:
  - Require that goalies wear appropriate equipment.
  - Establish a crease to protect the goalie (e.g., the size of a basketball key) and ensure that the goalie remains in the crease at all times during play.
  - Do not permit any other player or player's stick to enter the crease.

Educator Check and Reflect: Striking With Feet

- Encourage participants to kick or shoot the ball on an angle.
- Use groups of four or five to maximize ball contact.
- Encourage participants to develop critical thinking skills by focusing on game strategies throughout the activity.
- Caution participants to be aware of objects and people around them.
- Refer to administration policy regarding heading. If heading is permitted, remind participants that heading does not hurt when performed correctly.
- Ensure that balls not in play are retrieved from the activity area immediately to avoid injuries.

HOCKEY CIRCLE RELAY

Activity Goal

To maintain control of the object while circling the group as quickly as possible.

Fundamental Movement Skills

Striking with an implement, running

Tactical Focus

Offense: Maintain possession.

Level

Beginning

Facility

Gymnasium

Equipment

8 to 10 small objects (e.g., foam balls, rings, beanbags), 20 to 30 foam hockey sticks (1 per participant)

Time
15 to 20 minutes

Activity Category
Territory

Safety
Keep groups a safe distance from walls and each other. Remind participants to keep their heads up to be aware of objects and other participants.

Activity Instructions
Groups of five or six form circles and number off; each participant has a stick. The first participant dribbles an object around the outside of the circle, returns to the starting place, and passes the object for the second participant to dribble around the circle. While participants circle the group, the remaining participants pass a second object around in the circle while waiting their turns to dribble. For the second round, consider calling out numbers randomly; the participant with the corresponding number dribbles around the circle. If equipment is limited, consider using only two sticks and one small object per group.

Adaptations
To decrease the challenge:
- Decrease the size of the circle.
- Allow participants to select the objects they dribble.
- Use beanbags.

To increase the challenge:
- Increase the size of the circle.
- Set a period of time in which each participant must complete the dribble.
- Require participants to use their nondominant hands.

Self-Check Questions
- Do I keep my head up when dribbling?
- Do I make small, quick passes?
- Am I controlling the object as I dribble around the circle?
- Do I follow through when I release the object toward my teammate?

BLADE TARGETS

Activity Goal

To maintain control of an object.

Fundamental Movement Skill

Striking with an implement

Tactical Focus

Offense: Maintain possession.

Level

Beginning

Facility

Gymnasium or outdoors

Equipment

10 to 15 small objects (e.g., foam balls, foam rings, beanbags), 20 to 30 foam hockey sticks (1 per participant)

Time

20 to 25 minutes

Activity Category

Territory

Safety

Keep partners and groups a safe distance from walls and each other. Remind participants to keep their heads up to be aware of objects and other participants.

Activity Instructions

Working in pairs with foam hockey sticks and one object of their choice, partners pass the object, aiming for their partners' blades. After a successful pass, partners increase the challenge by increasing the distance between them. Continue the activity for an appropriate amount of time.

During the second round, groups of five or six form circles and pass an object across the circle aiming for group members' blades. Encourage them to stop the object with their sticks before passing it to another participant.

Adaptations

To decrease the challenge:

- Permit pairs to select the objects they dribble.
- Decrease the size of the circle in round 2.

To increase the challenge:

- Require participants to use their nondominant hands.
- Increase the size of the circle in round 2.
- Add another ball in round 2.

Self-Check Questions

- Am I aiming my pass at my partner's blade?
- Do I use a smooth, sweeping motion with a follow-through toward my partner?
- Do I keep my eyes on the ball when receiving a pass?
- Do I follow through when I release the object toward my partner?

SQUARED OUT

Activity Goal

To maintain control of the ball while circling the group as quickly as possible.

Fundamental Movement Skill

Dribbling

Tactical Focus

- Offense: Maintain possession.
- Defense: Defend space.

Level

Beginning

Facility

Gymnasium or outdoors

Equipment

10 to 12 balls (various sizes)

Time

15 to 20 minutes

Activity Category

Territory

Safety

Keep groups a safe distance from walls and from each other. Remind participants to keep their heads up to be aware of balls and other participants as they dribble.

Activity Instructions

Divide participants into groups of six, and give each group two balls. Four group members make a square (in a size that offers an optimal challenge level); the remaining two members, each with a ball, are on the outside of the square. The outside players dribble their balls with their feet around the square in the same direction and attempt to tag each other. Consider having participants in the square perform a physical task (e.g., jumping jack, squat) while counting. Once a player is tagged, all players switch roles. Be sure to switch roles often.

Adaptations

To decrease the challenge:

- Decrease the size of the square.
- Use a different type of ball.
- Provide equipment so participants can dribble in different ways (e.g., with hands in basketball, with a stick in hockey).

To increase the challenge:

- Increase the size of the square.
- Require that participants use their nondominant hands.
- Have participants in the square attempt to intercept the dribbling of the outside players.

Self-Check Questions

- Do I keep my head up while dribbling?
- Do I use one hand to protect the ball?
- Do I make quick decisions while moving with the ball?

Activity Goal

To maintain control of the ball while overtaking the opponent's ball.

Fundamental Movement Skill

Kicking

Tactical Focus

Offense: Maintain possession.

Level

Exploring

Facility

Gymnasium or outdoors

Equipment

10 to 12 balls (various sizes)

Time

15 to 20 minutes

Activity Category

Territory

Safety

Keep groups a safe distance from walls and each other. Remind participants to keep their heads up to be aware of balls and other participants.

Activity Instructions

Groups of six separate into two teams of three. All six participants form one large circle, alternating teammates. One participant from each team starts with a ball at different sides of the circle. Both teams kick their balls clockwise to their own teammates around the circle, passing to every other person, receiving the ball from the teammate on the left, and trapping it before passing it along to the teammate on the right. Teams score 1 point every time their ball passes an opponent's ball.

Adaptations

To decrease the challenge:

- Decrease the size of the circle.
- Provide larger balls.
- Have participants roll or throw balls before progressing to kicking them.

To increase the challenge:

- Increase the size of the circle.
- Allow participants to send balls in different ways (e.g., with their nondominant feet or with an implement).
- Add a defender who attempts to intercept the passes.

Self-Check Questions

- Do I keep my hip and knee bent during my backswing?
- Do I use the required amount of force to send the ball to teammates?
- Do I contact the ball with my instep or laces?
- Do I follow through toward my teammates when I kick the ball?

TEAM CROQUET

Activity Goal

To use an implement to project a ball accurately to a target.

Fundamental Movement Skill

Striking with an implement

Tactical Focus

Offense: Determine an appropriate distance from which to throw an object, avoid obstacles.

Level

Exploring

Facility

Gymnasium

Equipment

4 to 6 soft skin balls (various sizes), 4 to 6 foam hockey sticks, 9 cones

Time

25 to 30 minutes

Activity Category

Target

Safety

Keep cones a safe distance from walls and from each other. Remind participants to keep their heads up to be aware of balls being struck throughout the activity space.

Activity Instructions

Use cones to mark nine targets throughout the activity space, and number them from 1 to 9.

Each group of four to six has one ball and one hockey stick and lines up at a target. Group members adopt a wide-legged stance to act as a tunnel in front of the cone. Members then take turns striking the ball through the teammates' legs toward the cone in an attempt to reach the cone in the least number of turns. The member farthest away from the cone strikes first. Each member strikes once, leaves the ball where it lands, passes the hockey stick to the next member, and returns to their spot in line. Consider having groups keep track of the number of shots they took to reach each cone. Once groups have reached a cone, they move to the next one until they have completed all nine targets.

Adaptations

To decrease the challenge:

- Decrease the distance between the teammates standing as gates.
- Allow participants to send the ball with their hands or feet.

To increase the challenge:

- Increase the distance between the teammates standing as gates.
- Keep individual scores instead of team scores.
- Have teammates use a narrow stance.

Self-Check Questions

- Do I strike the ball proficiently toward the target?
- Do I apply the required amount of force to get the ball to the target?
- Am I able to manipulate the ball with spins to avoid obstacles?

ONE-END SOCCER

Activity Goal

To score goals into the opponents' net.

Fundamental Movement Skills

Kicking, dribbling, trapping

Tactical Focus

- Offense: Maintain possession, create space, attack the goal.
- Defense: Regain possession, defend the goal.

Level

Exploring

Facility

Gymnasium or outdoors

Equipment

3 to 5 balls (various sizes), 3 to 5 nets or 6 to 10 cones (for goals)

Time

20 to 25 minutes

Activity Category

Territory

Safety

Keep games a safe distance from walls and from each other. Remind participants to keep their heads up to be aware of balls and other participants as they move throughout the activity space.

Activity Instructions

Divide participants into teams of four to six and pair up teams for games. Offensive teams have one extra player. Each playing area has only one goal in the end zone. The offensive team tries to pass to an open player before scoring, while the defensive team attempts to intercept. After each point or interception, the offensive team maintains possession for three to five minutes of play before the additional player moves to the defensive team as that team becomes the offensive team. As required, pause the game to ensure that the additional player has moved to the correct team.

Adaptations

To decrease the challenge:

- Decrease the size of the activity area.
- Change the type of ball (e.g., soft skin ball).
- Use more than one ball in each game.

To increase the challenge:

- Increase the size of the activity area.
- Keep individual scores instead of team scores.
- Require that players send the ball in different ways (e.g., with their nondominant feet or with an implement).

Self-Check Questions

- Do I keep my head up while dribbling?
- Do I move to an open space to receive the ball?
- Do I apply the required amount of force to send the ball to teammates or to the goal?
- Do I follow through toward my target when I release the ball?

GIVE-AND-GO

Activity Goal

To score goals following a give-and-go.

Fundamental Movement Skills

Kicking, dribbling, trapping

Tactical Focus

- Offense: Maintain possession, create space, attack the goal.
- Defense: Regain possession, defend the goal.

Level

Exploring

Facility

Gymnasium or outdoors

Equipment

10 to 12 balls (various sizes)

Time

15 to 20 minutes

Activity Category

Territory

Safety

Keep groups a safe distance from walls and each other. Remind participants to keep their heads up to be aware of balls and other participants as they move throughout the activity space.

Activity Instructions

Participants create groups of three and practice the give-and-go with imaginary defenders. Player 1 passes to player 2 and runs toward the goal; player 2 traps the ball and then passes it back to player 1, who is now in front of the goal. Player 1 takes a shot on player 3, who is in the goal trying to block the shot. Players change roles after each play.

Next, groups pair up to practice the give-and-go against defenders in mini-games. Teams receive 1 point for scoring and 2 points for scoring after performing a give-and-go. Players switch positions often.

Adaptations

To decrease the challenge:

- Decrease the size of the playing area.
- Add a second ball to maximize participation.
- Change the type of ball (e.g., foam ball).

To increase the challenge:

- Increase the size of the playing area.
- Keep individual scores instead of team scores.
- Add an additional score for accuracy from a distance.

Self-Check Questions

- Do I apply the required amount of force to send the ball to my teammates during the give-and-go?
- Do I move to an open space to receive the ball?
- Do I follow through toward the goal when I release the ball?

UNEVEN KEEP-AWAY

Activity Goal

To maintain possession of the ball.

Fundamental Movement Skills

Kicking, dribbling, trapping

Tactical Focus

- Offense: Maintain possession, create space.
- Defense: Defend space, regain possession.

Level

Competent

Facility

Gymnasium or outdoors

Equipment

6 to 10 balls (various sizes)

Time

20 to 25 minutes

Activity Category

Territory

Safety

Keep games a safe distance from walls and each other. Remind participants to keep their heads up to be aware of balls and other participants
as they move throughout the activity space.

Activity Instructions

Participants form teams of three to five and play mini-games of keep-
away with uneven teams (e.g., 3v4 or 4v5). The team with the extra
player begins in offense with possession of the ball and attempts to
keep the ball away from the defensive team by passing to the open
player. Switch offensive and defensive roles often, including the extra
player. Encourage teams to keep track of their consecutive passes by
counting out loud.

Adaptations

To decrease the challenge:
- Decrease the size of the playing area.
- Change the type of ball (e.g., soft skin ball).
- Add more than one ball to maximize participation.

To increase the challenge:
- Increase the size of the playing area.
- Change the mode of passing (e.g., bounce, kick).
- Modify the method of dribbling (e.g., hockey stick and ball, soccer
  balls and feet).

Self-Check Questions

- Do I keep my head up while dribbling?
- Do I move to an open space to receive the ball?
- Do I apply the required amount of force to send the ball to the
  designated space?
- Do I follow through toward my target when I release the ball?

SHORT- AND LONG-BASE KICK BASEBALL

Activity Goal

To score as many runs as possible.

Fundamental Movement Skill

Kicking

Tactical Focus

- Offense: Kick accurately, score runs, avoid getting out.
- Defense: Stop runs from scoring, make hitting the ball difficult.

Level

Competent

Facility

Outdoors

Equipment

3 bases and 1 ball (various sizes) per game

Time

20 to 25 minutes

Activity Category

Striking/fielding

Safety

Check outdoor activity spaces for tripping hazards (e.g., holes, objects); remove or mark any hazards. Provide a safe distance between games occurring in the same space. Remind participants to keep their heads up to be aware of balls and participants moving throughout the activity space.

Activity Instructions

Participants divide into teams of four or five and pair up to play games in areas that include a home base, a short first base, and a long second base. Participants place the bases at what they believe to be optimally challenging distances.

The pitcher on the defending team rolls the ball to the offensive player on home base, who kicks it. The kicker runs to either the short base for 1 point or the long base for 2 points. The kicker is out if a fly ball is caught by the defensive team or if the ball is returned to home base by the defensive team before the kicker lands on either the short or the long base. Teams switch places once all offensive participants have had a turn kicking.

Adaptations

To decrease the challenge:

- Decrease the distance between the bases.
- Increase the size of the ball.
- Allow offensive players to strike with an implement (e.g., foam hockey stick).

To increase the challenge:

- Increase the distance between the bases.
- Keep individual scores instead of team scores.
- Change the method of locomotion (e.g., skip, hop, gallop).

Self-Check Questions

- Do I cover space while in the outfield?
- Do I apply the required amount of force to send the ball to the designated target?
- Do I move quickly in the outfield to stop runs from scoring?
- Do I use critical thinking skills to determine which base to run to?

FIVE-MINUTE MINI-GAME

Activity Goal

To score goals.

Fundamental Movement Skills

Kicking, dribbling, trapping

Tactical Focus

- Offense: Maintain possession, create space, attack the goal.
- Defense: Defend space, defend the goal, regain possession.

Level

Competent

Facility

Gymnasium or outdoors

Equipment

6 to 8 balls (various sizes), 8 to 12 cones

Time

20 to 25 minutes

Activity Category

Territory

Safety

Keep games a safe distance from walls and each other. Remind participants to keep their heads up to be aware of balls and other participants as they move throughout the activity space.

Activity Instructions

Participants form teams of four or five and play a modified game of soccer. Each playing space has a goal (designated with cones) in each end zone. Participants select their initial on-field positions, such as goalie (one), defense (one), midfield (one), and forward (two). After one minute of play, teammates switch positions and play continues. After five minutes all participants should have had a chance to play each position. Teams switch opponents and restart the one-minute timing for the new game.

Adaptations

To decrease the challenge:

- Decrease the size of the playing area.
- Change the type of ball (e.g., soft skin ball).
- Add more than one ball to maximize participation.

To increase the challenge:

- Increase the size of the playing area.
- Modify the method of dribbling (e.g., hockey stick and ball).
- Add a second defense position, and do not use a goalie.

Self-Check Questions
- Do I move to an open space to receive the ball?
- Do I communicate with my teammates?
- Do I apply the required amount of force to send the ball to the designated target?
- Do I recognize openings in play and scoring opportunities?

HOLD FAST

Activity Goal
To maintain possession of the ring.

Fundamental Movement Skills
Striking with an implement, trapping

Tactical Focus
- Offense: Create space.
- Defense: Defend space.

Level
Competent

Facility
Gymnasium or outdoors

Equipment
25 to 30 ringette sticks or hockey stick shafts (1 per participant), 6 or 8 foam or rubber rings, 20 to 30 cones

Time
15 to 20 minutes

Activity Category
Territory

Safety

Keep groups a safe distance from walls and each other. Remind participants to keep their heads up to be aware of rings being passed and participants moving throughout the activity area.

Activity Instructions

Working in groups of four, three players attempt to maintain possession of the ring while passing it back and forth; the fourth player tries to intercept it, collecting 1 point if successful. Following an interception, players switch roles. Change interceptors often.

Adaptations

To decrease the challenge:

- Decrease the size of the playing area.
- Use multiple rings per game.
- Remove the sticks and have players kick a ball (e.g., soccer ball).

To increase the challenge:

- Increase the size of the activity area.
- Add a time limit in which the interception must happen before players rotate.
- Have two participants trying to intercept the ring.

Self-Check Questions

- Am I able to trap and pass the ring quickly?
- Do I move to an open space to receive the ring?
- Do I follow through toward my teammate when I release the ring?
- Do I apply the right amount of force to send the ring to my teammate?

WALL BALL SOCCER

Activity Goal

To score points by kicking the ball against the opposing team's wall.

Fundamental Movement Skills

Kicking, dribbling, trapping

Tactical Focus

- Offense: Maintain possession, create space, attack the goal, set plays.
- Defense: Regain possession, defend the goal, set plays.

Level

Proficient

Facility

Gymnasium

Equipment

2 to 4 balls (various sizes), walls in close proximity to each other, 4 to 8 cones

Time

20 to 25 minutes

Activity Category

Territory

Safety

Provide a safe distance between games occurring in the same space. Remind participants to keep their heads up to be aware of balls and other participants in the activity space.

Activity Instructions

Participants form groups of four to six and pair up to play soccer against one wall. Teams use cones to mark an end zone along one wall where the defending team may stand. The offensive team attempts to score by kicking the ball against the defensive team's wall, below waist height and between the cones. Following a point, the other team gets possession of the ball and they switch roles, the defensive team now becomes offensive, and tries to score on the area they were just protecting.

Adaptations

To decrease the challenge:

- Decrease the size of the scoring area between cones.
- Use nets for goals.
- Change the type of ball (e.g., soft skin ball).

To increase the challenge:

- Increase the size of the scoring area between cones.
- Modify the method of dribbling (e.g., ball and hockey stick, basketball and hands).
- Limit the number of times players can pass the ball before attempting to score.

Self-Check Questions

- Do I move to an open space to receive the ball?
- Do I communicate my position with my teammates?
- Do I use passing and faking strategies to find open space?

ZONE RINGETTE

Activity Goal

To score as many points as possible.

Fundamental Movement Skills

Striking, dribbling, trapping

Tactical Focus

- Offense: Create space, attack the goal, set plays.
- Defense: Set plays, defend the goal, defend space.

Level

Proficient

Facility

Gymnasium or outdoors

Equipment

25 to 30 ringette sticks or hockey stick shafts (1 per participant), 2 or 3 foam rings, 20 to 30 cones

Time

25 to 30 minutes

Activity Category

Territory

Safety

Keep games a safe distance from walls and from each other. Remind participants to keep their heads up to be aware of rings being passed and participants moving throughout the activity area.

Activity Instructions

Participants divide into equal teams of 4 to 6, and pair up to compete. Divide playing areas into the same number of zones as there are players so that all players have their own zones. Mark zones with cones and create goals at each end of the playing area with cones. Using their sticks, players pass the ring to teammates in an attempt to score; they may not leave their zones. After a point is scored, all players rotate zones.

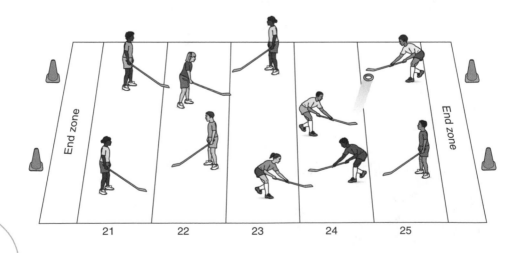

Adaptations

To decrease the challenge:

- Decrease the number of zones.
- Use multiple rings.
- Remove the implement and have players use a ball (e.g., soccer ball).

To increase the challenge:

- Increase the number of zones.
- Add a time limit in which points must be scored before all players rotate.
- Require that teams pass the ring to each player before attempting to score.

Self-Check Questions

- Am I able to trap and pass the ring quickly?
- Do I move to an open space to receive the ring?
- Do I follow through toward my teammate or the goal when I release the ring?
- Do I apply the right amount of force to send the ring to a teammate or the goal?

CAPTIVE HOCKEY

Activity Goal

To score more points than the opposing team.

Fundamental Movement Skills

Striking, dribbling, trapping

Tactical Focus

- Offense: Create space, attack the goal, set plays.
- Defense: Defend the goal, defend space, set plays.

Level

Proficient

Facility

Gymnasium or outdoors

Equipment

5 to 7 small balls (e.g., tennis balls, sponge balls, foam balls), 20 to 30 sticks (1 per participant), 4 to 6 cones or nets (for goals)

Time

15 to 20 minutes

Activity Category

Territory

Safety

Keep games a safe distance from walls and each other. Remind participants to keep their heads up to be aware of balls being passed and other participants moving throughout the activity space.

Activity Instructions

Participants divide into equal teams of 4 to 6, and pair up for games. Use cones or nets to create goals at either end of each playing area. Using their sticks, participants pass to teammates to advance the ball in an attempt to score. After a point is scored, one player from the opposing team moves to the scoring team. Points are tracked by seeing how many players have changed teams. The game continues until one team has captured all of the opposing team's players.

Adaptations

To decrease the challenge:

- Create smaller playing areas.
- Use multiple balls.
- Add a time limit after which all players must return to their original teams.

To increase the challenge:

- Create larger playing areas.
- Add a time limit in which points must be scored.
- Require that teams pass the ball to each player before attempting to score.

Self-Check Questions

- Am I able to trap and pass the ball quickly?
- Do I move to an open space to receive the ball?
- Do I follow through toward my teammate or the goal after releasing the ball?
- Do I apply the right amount of force to send the ball to my teammate or the goal?

About the Author

Heather Gardner, MEd, is a curriculum consultant in Toronto with decades of experience in public school teaching and as a provincial health and physical education (HPE) consultant. She has done major curriculum consulting work for Ophea, a not-for-profit organization that champions healthy, active living in schools and communities. She has been an HPE teacher and curriculum consultant for the Hamilton Wentworth District School Board. Gardner also has been an HPE instructor for Brock University in St. Catharines, Ontario, and has served as a writer and instructor for the Elementary Teacher Federation of Ontario. She was honored by *Best Health* magazine as having Canada's best fitness blog in 2013. Gardner enjoys running, yoga, and participating in half Ironman triathlons.

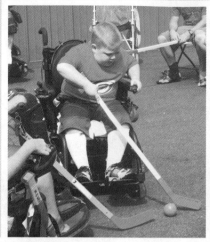

You'll find other outstanding
physical education resources at

www.HumanKinetics.com

In the U.S. call 1.800.747.4457
Canada. 1.800.465.7301
Europe . . . . +44 (0) 113 255 5665

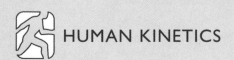

HUMAN KINETICS